Jason -
Thank you
for being the kind of person who is committed
to changing
what doesn't
work in the world.

Much love,

IMPACT FOUNDER

KRISTIN DARGA

DENVER, CO

For the three founders whose passing inspired me to start Impact Founder, their legacy motivates me daily to continue this work and make a difference in our community so that founders don't feel isolated or alone in their experience. For their friends and families who in their absence, experience a loss, may you know their legacy lives in our stories and in changing the face of entrepreneurship.

Josh Greenberg, Grooveshark (April 17, 1987 - July 19, 2015)
Faigy Mayer, Appton (1986 - July 20, 2015)
Austen Heinz, Cambrian Genomics (1983 - May 24, 2015)

And for my parents, for all the brainstorm sessions and tears they've endured, who believe in my dreams and vision no matter the circumstances. I love you both.

CONTENTS

CONTENTS

TESTIMONIALS

"This is a book about generosity and about boundaries. The generosity to build something bigger than yourself, and to do it for other people. And the boundaries that are required to do it without losing yourself and your life in the process." - *Seth Godin, Author of Linchpin*

"We need to become more vulnerable and practice vulnerability. Living a true and authentic life will actually open up more doors, instead of closing them. Why can I go to a happy hour and say 'I just had the most killer arm exercise at the gym.' Why can't I go to that same happy hour and say 'I just had the most incredible hour with my therapist?' Why is that a stigma in our culture? That's one thing that keeps me very passionate about what we're doing with Catalyst, that we need to demystify all of that. This is why I so deeply believe in Impact Founder's mission, as they are helping communities with this exact initiative." - *Mike Biselli, Catalyst HTI*

"In the entrepreneurial world where most people talk about the successes and wins, it is extremely important to address the real and difficult issues most founders face on the way there. Impact Founder addresses these in the most honest, candid, and inspiring way possible through real stories seldom discussed. The community Impact Founder is fostering around shared stories of overcoming struggle helps entrepreneurs deal with their respective issues that we all inevitably face building companies." - *Sam Tarantino, Chromatic FM*

"Impact Founder has opened my eyes as a fellow entrepreneur that it's all right to falter. I have celebrated some of my life's biggest successes as an entrepreneur and weeks later had to overcome some of my largest failures - these stories have helped me realized that I'm not an anomaly. I'm not just another entrepreneur in the sea of challenges. In a way, these people and their stories have given me hope. I know now that it's all worth fighting for, that there is a light at the end of the tunnel and that light is a successful business!" - *Michelle Marie King, Founder of Positive Presence, LLC*

"Founders struggling with the ups and downs of building a company that makes a meaningful difference on the planet will find solace in these pages. The stories in Impact Founder reveal touching portraits of others walking the path and finding their humanity along the way. " - *Kati Bicknell, Co-founder of Kindara*

"My heart is so aligned and filled with gratitude for this work. Kristin and her team are pioneering a much-needed reminder of what is deeply needed in the world today - deep connection. I am such a profound supporter of Impact Founder and connecting global thought leaders worldwide. Impact Founder is a powerful energy in motion for global collaboration and connection." - *Leanne Jacobs, Founder of HealthyGirl + Author of Beautiful Money*

FOREWORD

While there is nothing wrong with celebrating triumphs, solely focusing on them in our daily interactions usually leads to relationships lacking connection and meaning. I first met Kristin and Impact Founder in the fall of 2016 after a particularly traumatic transition period in my life. My online business of 9 years, which had 30 million users and 100 employees, collapsed, followed a few months later by the death of my co-founder and best friend, Josh Greenberg. I had just given a speech on how failures and deaths like the one I had recently endured propel us to become stronger than our successes.

Kristin and I spoke at length about how Josh's passing had inspired her to begin compiling stories that are never told: the ones about the difficulties we face throughout our entrepreneurial journeys. The times that almost compel us to quit and what fire drives us to keep going. In my case, even after having lost the business and the person that created my entire career and identity, my fire was incidentally the root of my sadness in Josh's passing.

I learned a lot from the way Josh approached life. Josh had grown up without a father figure. What always impressed me most over the years was that rather than mope about it, he learned to code as a kid, and by his teens was selling websites to clients to help his family make ends meet.

When he and I started Grooveshark in Gainesville, Florida together it was virtually impossible to hire engineers. So Josh spearheaded an initiative around town to help train people to learn to code just as he had. At Grooveshark, 90% of our staff had been trained in this way. This relentless sense of duty, of working towards a greater goal to help others despite seemingly impossible odds, is what defined Josh's life as well as Grooveshark's, and continues to be instrumental in my continued evolution as an entrepreneur.

Impact Founder is a channel for stories like these; of duty and overcoming the odds in today's environment of self-congratulating successes. Kristin pinpoints the fire within each entrepreneur that keeps them going and brings it to the well-deserved center stage. She illustrates the fragile, true nature of our individual egos and how our greatest failures are the real source of our inspirations and eventual successes. May these stories help cross the chasm of doubt that we all inevitably face in the pursuit of meaning and achievement.

Sam Tarantino
Co-founder, Grooveshark

A LETTER FROM OUR FOUNDER

"I was on the phone with the suicide prevention hotline for my boyfriend, a depressed and overwhelmed business founder."

I am on a mission to make sure we never lose another entrepreneur due to isolation, feelings of inadequacy, failure, or for any other reason. Self-doubt is part of life and sometimes entrepreneurs face the issue alone, and lose their perspective. As the leader of a movement to build real entrepreneurship – to empower entrepreneurs to keep making change in the world and to not give up - I know it is important to share vulnerably. This is the story of what lead me to create Impact Founder™.

In 2014, the relationship with my boyfriend at the time was ending and he was threatening to commit suicide. He told me why: he was overwhelmed, his business was growing too fast to keep up, and with everything that was happening between us, it had become unbearable and he didn't see a way out; he wanted to kill himself. He shared every detail as to how he had it planned, and thought that it would be easy, painless.

I was committed to doing what I could so I called the suicide prevention lifeline. Calling the lifeline was the single most important decision I made, and, as a result, I am grateful to say, he is still alive today. He is one of the lucky ones – I happened to be there at the right time and fortunately made the right call.

He created an incredible business. He developed an entirely new, efficient, high-quality product, and in less than a year his business had about 40% of the market share. He couldn't keep up. He was achieving his dream, but then felt totally overwhelmed and inadequate because he did not know how to keep up with the growth. We might expect those feelings when we fail, but here he was wildly succeeding and still felt unable to handle it.

Understanding that, I learned an extremely important lesson watching what he was going through as a success. I learned that everyone, absolutely EVERYONE, feels a certain level of inadequacy. No matter how someone appears to others, they are dealing with their own perceived set of internal shortcomings and often believe that they are the only ones with those shortcomings. That is simply not the truth.

Less than a year later, there were two suicides of startup founders and the sudden death of a third. Worst of all, all three were under the age of 32. When I read about Josh Greenberg (Grooveshark), Faigy Mayer (Appton), and Austen Heinz (Cambrian Genomics), I made the decision to do whatever I could to help alleviate the feeling of inadequacy, isolation, depression and suicide among founders by sharing real stories of real entrepreneurs' struggles and successes.

My goal is to create a network for entrepreneurs so they never feel isolated or inadequate. Sharing the real stories of real entrepreneurs helps all of us understand that we are not alone with the challenges. While being an entrepreneur will never be free of stress and self-doubt, my hope is that it will never lead to the devastating outcomes of Josh, Faigy or Austen.

Whenever I think of my experience that day, I am overcome with emotion. My saving grace was my community, and that's what motivated me to start Impact Founder.

We completed our initial launch in Denver with a photography exhibit at Denver Startup Week, September, 2015. In a single week, 7,000 entrepreneurs visited our exhibit. Next, we launched a way for any entrepreneur to submit their own audio story and photo. We did this so we could build a larger constituency and community of relatable stories. The mission is that all founders can share what is really happening in their lives and help reduce feelings of isolation for others. Our social impact is that founders are sharing authentically, creating a global conversation, and helping reduce depression and suicide in our community.

Please read on and join our movement.

Best,

Kristin Darga, Founder
ImpactFounder.com

AN INVITATION FOR YOU

I invite you to see yourself somewhere in this book and take solace in the fact that the people you are relating to survived to tell their stories. What this book accomplishes is a look at the range of issues from self-doubt to overwhelm to the internal battles of all kinds that entrepreneurs face. My ongoing research has also shown that the challenges are representative of entrepreneurs everywhere. It is my quest to create a platform where those stories can be shared. What's most fascinating to me is that at the time we interviewed the people in this book, it seemed from the outside that they were experiencing success. And yet there they were, at that moment, still filled with self-doubt.

I am reminded of the definition of courage that is often attributed to our military members... "It's not that we're not scared, it's that we did it anyway." And with that definition in mind, I invite you to come in and share the stories in the book, share your story on our platform, learn from others, help others learn from you, and let's create a real dialogue to make sure that what happened to the three entrepreneurs who inspired this book never happens again.

"WE HAD A SUCCESSFUL LAUNCH OF IMPACT FOUNDER IN JUST 7 WEEKS, AND I WAS CONFRONTED BY RESPONSIBILITY OF WHAT I BUILT."

KRISTIN
DARGA

Kristin Darga, Founder of Impact Founder™, is an executive coach who takes entrepreneurs to the next level, guiding and supporting them to break the code of what's holding them back. She coaches her clients, who are risking everything for what they believe in, how to keep persevering when burnout is mounting, ultimately empowering them to continue creating change in the world. According to Kristin, "As a business owner, I can't deny the direct correlation between my health and happiness and the growth of my business, and I set out to help people create the same synergy in their lives and businesses. I specialize in working with entrepreneurs and CEOs to build synergy between their personal health, business, and life."

Through her work, she saw need for a community where founders could connect and share their stories of success and failures. After her ex-boyfriend almost took his life and she heard about a number of founder suicides, Kristin took action and created Impact Founder, now a global multi-media movement to create authentic entrepreneurship community. This growing community supports and empowers entrepreneurs to combat isolation through connection and support each other through the struggles to make a lasting impact.

She has a multitude of experience as a founder, executive director, and manager with nonprofits, startups and corporations, including Sony Pictures Entertainment.

During her training, she studied with some of the world's top health and wellness experts at the Institute for Integrative Nutrition©. Including Dr. Andrew Weil, Director of the Arizona Center for Integrative Medicine; Dr. Deepak Chopra, leader in the field of mind-body medicine; Dr. David Katz, Director of Yale University's Prevention Research Center; Dr. Walter Willett, Chair of Nutrition at Harvard University. The program at the Institute for Integrative nutrition covers over 100 dietary theories, innovative coaching and practical lifestyle management techniques. She has also furthered her education by training with Landmark Worldwide.

Connect with Kristin for more information on Impact Founder, or to be featured as an Impact Founder, please visit: www.impactfounder.com To book Kristin for interviews, keynotes, or coaching email: impactfounderproject@gmail.com

ALONZO
MARTINEZ

OWNER
Komotodo Sushi Burrito

"BUSINESS IS OPENING
SOON AND I WILL NOT
HAVE ENOUGH MONEY
FOR PAYROLL."

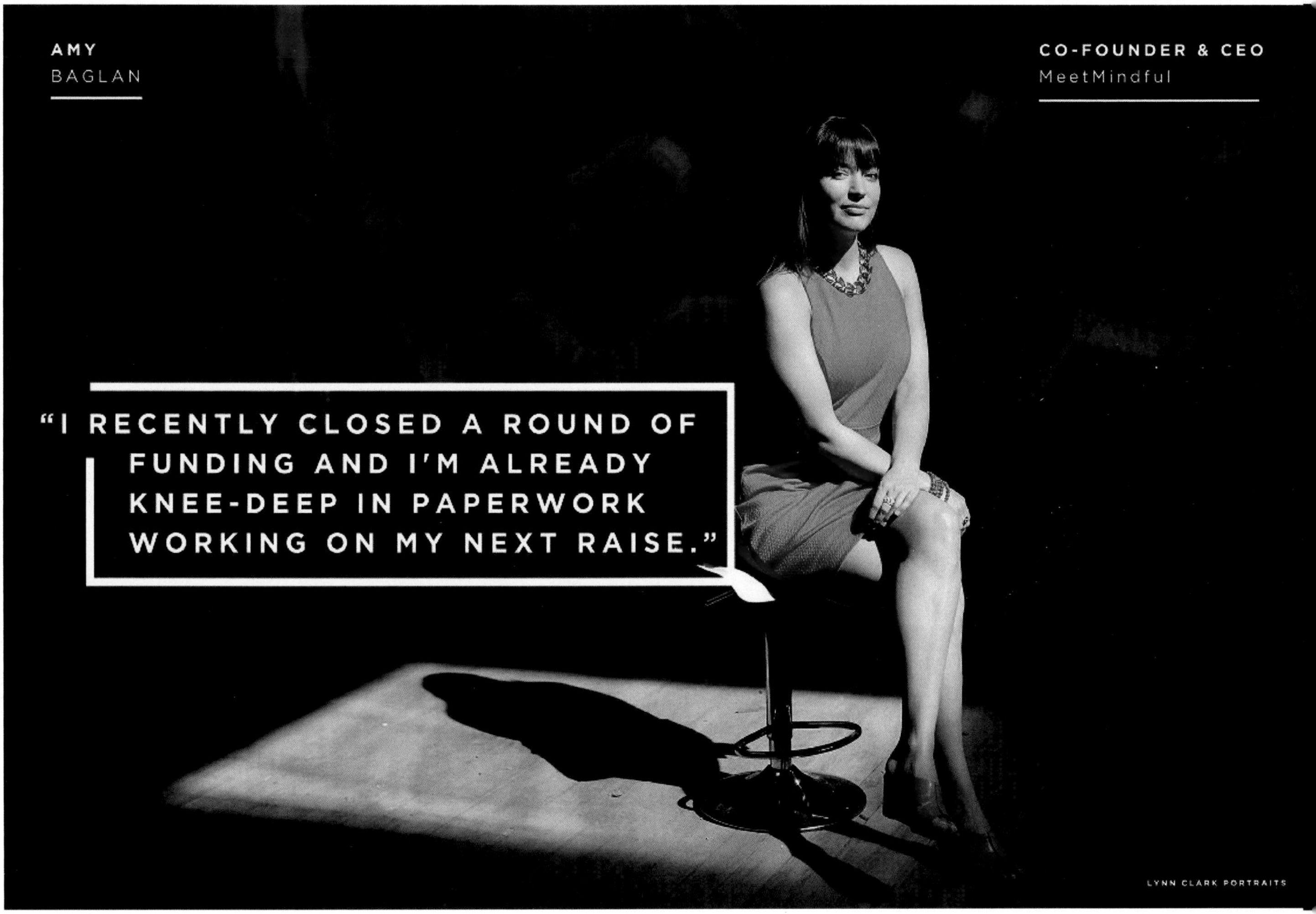

AMY
BAGLAN

CO-FOUNDER & CEO
MeetMindful

"I RECENTLY CLOSED A ROUND OF
FUNDING AND I'M ALREADY
KNEE-DEEP IN PAPERWORK
WORKING ON MY NEXT RAISE."

LYNN CLARK PORTRAITS

ANDREA
KUPFER

FOUNDER & CEO
Copper Lane

"I STARTED MY BUSINESS TO
SAVE MY MARRIAGE, ENDED
UP FILING FOR DIVORCE
AND MY CLIENTS TRIPLED. "

BARBARA ANDRI
MONDAY IOANNIDOU

CO-FOUNDERS
iscene llc

"WE BUILT A TOOL WE KNOW IS TRANSFORMING EDUCATION AND KIDS' LIVES GLOBALLY AND WE ARE ABOUT TO QUIT (BECAUSE WE CAN'T PAY THE RENT)."

'm Ann Kaemingk, an Executive Educator with LeleMarie. I became an entrepreneur because I needed a sense of control in my life. I was an elementary school teacher, had 28 fifth graders that I was working with and I would put in 50 to 60 hours a week. At that same time my husband and I were going through a fertility journey. So that sense of needing some control really spun out from those two paths overlapping. As an educator, I was not making more money each year because we were on a pay freeze and we had to pay more money for our pension and quite a bit more money for our health benefits. So, with all that extra work that I was putting in, and going to classes at night and developing things on the weekends, it didn't feel like I was being rewarded.

And then on the other side, we had unexplained infertility. It feels like having a baby should be the most natural thing in the world; that when you decide that it's time to create a family it would just happen. I was about to go through my third IVF (in vitro fertilization). So not only did I feel like I didn't have control because I couldn't get pregnant, but then my life was controlled by outside factors like all the doctor's appointments I had to go to, the injections that I had to do, the medications, the tests, the two-week waits, the months that we would have to take off, coupled with that feeling of being trapped in my classroom and not being rewarded for growth.

My biggest challenge as an entrepreneur has been myself. I think that you call it impostor syndrome. You wonder, "When is somebody going to figure out that I just don't know what I'm doing?"

My biggest challenge has just been believing in myself that I am capable of doing this and that I deserve to be successful. My biggest success so far in my entrepreneur journey has been the self-development that I've done, the self-confidence that I've gained. I feel extremely lucky that now I actually have had that story, this journey, because I have met some of the most amazing people in my life through my business. And they really launched my trajectory and put me on a completely different path than I would have ever dreamed of for myself.

The best advice I ever received was, "You are constantly reweaving the fabric of your life. Even the ugly, scary threads that we add to it, when you step back it's a beautiful tapestry that when we're up close and personal we can't see."

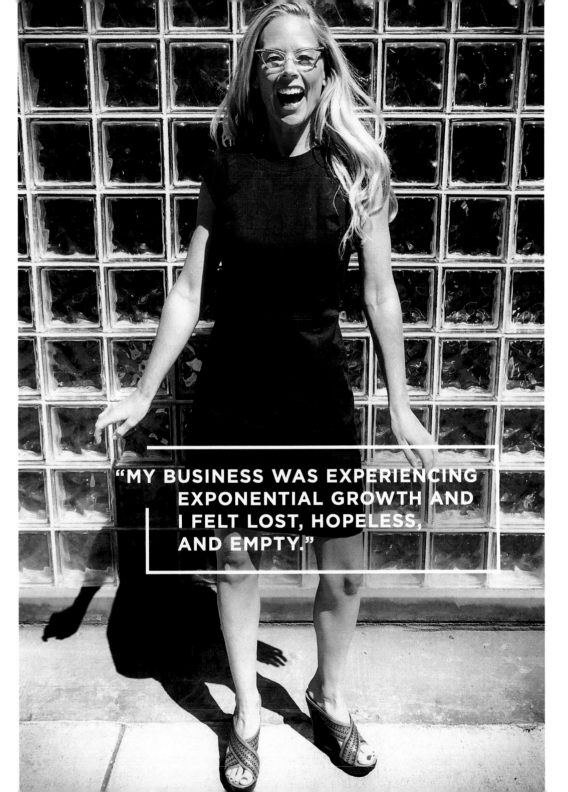

"MY BUSINESS WAS EXPERIENCING
EXPONENTIAL GROWTH AND
I FELT LOST, HOPELESS,
AND EMPTY."

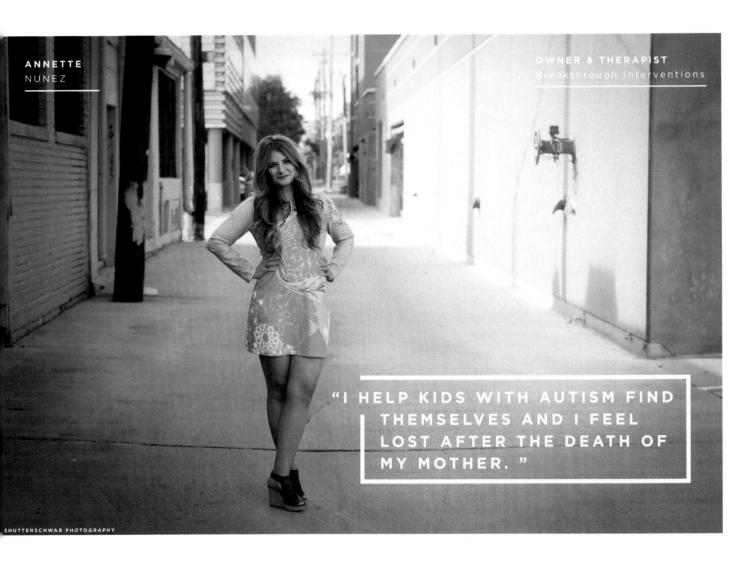

ANNETTE
NUNEZ

OWNER & THERAPIST
Breakthrough interventions

"I HELP KIDS WITH AUTISM FIND THEMSELVES AND I FEEL LOST AFTER THE DEATH OF MY MOTHER."

ANTHONY
FRANCO

FOUNDER, CEO
EffectiveUI & mc squares

"I'VE SOLD FIVE SUCCESSFUL COMPANIES AND I HAVEN'T HAD ONE CHAMPAGNE CORK MOMENT."

LYNN CLARK PORTRAIT

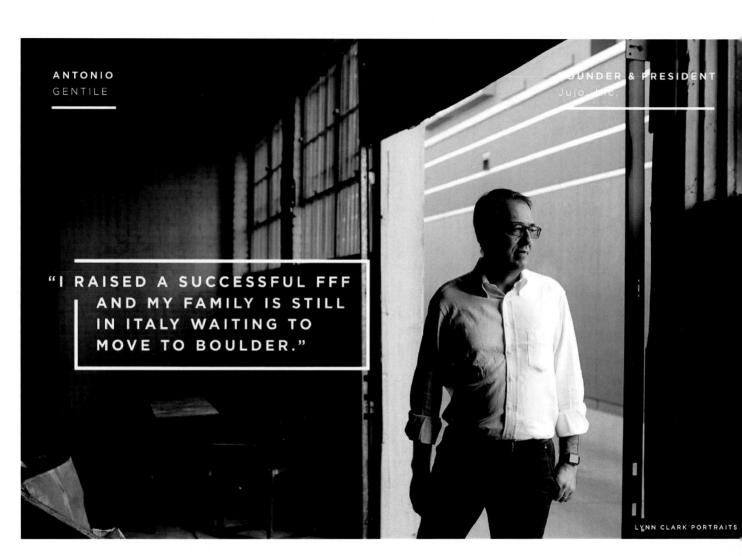

ANTONIO
GENTILE

FOUNDER & PRESIDENT
Jujo Inc.

"I RAISED A SUCCESSFUL FFF
AND MY FAMILY IS STILL
IN ITALY WAITING TO
MOVE TO BOULDER."

"I'VE SOLD TENS OF THOUSANDS OF DOLLARS WORTH OF PRODUCT AND STILL WONDER IF I'LL BE ABLE TO PAY RENT AT THE END OF EACH MONTH."

ARMAND
PIECUCH

My name is Armand Piecuch and I am Vice-President of Production at my company Fourth Wall Production. I became an entrepreneur because I wanted to be my own boss and I wanted to create a company culture within my industry and field that promoted growth as well as acceptance and an environment of non-prejudice against anyone who was involved and with us in our journey.

The biggest challenge was just to find a place here in Denver to really break into the market. Denver is such a bustling metropolis full of creative minds and individuals, it's been a challenge to just get noticed and be recognized and acknowledged for all the hard work and efforts that we put into every single one of our projects.

My biggest success as a company owner was to land a contract that produced a documentary about Bill Coors, the grandson of Adolph Coors, founder of the Coors Brewing Company. It was an amazing experience and provided us some amazing insight into our industry, as well as those who digest media and who create incredible stories that are worthy of being told through media.

The best advice I ever received was from a previous internship mentor. He said, "Do what you have to do until you can do what you want to do." That advice has resonated with me for years, and I tell myself that every day and I repeat it to everybody to encourage us to continue pushing forward towards a goal that we know will be well worth it.

BARBARA
MONDAY

CO-FOUNDER
iscene LLC

"I AM A STRONG, DRIVEN WOMAN
(WITH BOUNDLESS ENERGY)
CHANGING THE LIVES OF
KIDS ALL OVER THE WORLD
AND I AM EXHAUSTED BY
CHASING THE MONEY."

BRAD
TODD

FOUNDER + DESIGNER
Habitat

"I FINALLY FOUND A CAREER I WAS PASSIONATE ABOUT AND HAD TO FIGHT TO SAVE MY MARRIAGE."

My name is Brad Feld, and I'm a partner at a venture capital firm called Foundry Group, and I am also a co-founder of Techstars. I am an active investor as well as involved in a number of different companies. I first became an entrepreneur as a result of my father, who is medical doctor. As a kid my dad introduced me to a number of his patients who were entrepreneurs. A couple of them took me under their wings as mentors and I got exposed as a teenager who was a typical computer nerd in the late 70s and early 80s to a bunch of the early generation of entrepreneurs around personal computers. By the time I was a freshman in college I was already involved in a number of startups.

The biggest challenge over the years as an entrepreneur has been maintaining a high intensity of activity while continuing to have good emotional health. It's a continuous struggle to get to a good place but not overdo it and not run out of steam. I struggled through that period of time with my own understanding of myself. One of the things I'm most proud of is the work that I've done to be able to maintain a super-high-intensity focus on the work that I'm doing with a high level of engagement. Being able to know that I need to take some time for myself, back off from what I'm doing and create some space so I have the energy to keep going. My most significant accomplishment as an entrepreneur is my relationship with my wife Amy. I'm very happy that through all of that activity I've been able to create and be involved in a very healthy, long-term, successful relationship. If I gave advice to entrepreneurs I would make it very simple. You get one shot on this planet, make sure that what you're spending time on is something that you're obsessed about, something that you really care about, the people that you're with are people who you want to be with. You'll have struggles; there's lots of ups and downs. We're humans, we have lots of conflict. So be in the place and with the people you want to build your life around rather than you simply going someplace because you think there's an opportunity.

So use that frame of reference as an entrepreneur, because the beauty of it is that you can create what you want rather than have to do something that's imposed upon you.

"AT 47 MY BUSINESS WAS PERFORMING WELL, AND I HAD A SIGNIFICANT DEPRESSIVE EPISODE THAT LASTED SIX MONTHS."

BROCK
PREDOVICH

FOUNDER
IGNITRR

"I'M A FEW STEPS AWAY FROM ACHIEVING A LIFE GOAL OF CREATING A VENTURE CAPITAL FUND AND I JUST HAD MY HEART UTTERLY BROKEN IN A DIFFICULT DIVORCE."

LYNN CLARK PORTRAITS

CAMERON
POWELL

CEO
Physician Cognition

"I AM STILL GRIEVING THE
DEATH OF MY MOTHER AND
AM ALSO IN FLOW FOR THE
FIRST TIME IN YEARS."

CAMERON
SMITH

I'm Cameron Smith, the Founder and CEO of SquirrelBox Storage. I became an entrepreneur because I was constantly frustrated by the constraints of slow bureaucracy and big corporations and government. And I actually wanted to use the full scope of my skills and abilities to solve painful problems. Furthermore, I wanted to lead teams of people and lead them well.

My biggest challenge in being an entrepreneur is getting up each morning knowing that I need to keep pushing through the really tough, bleak times. So much of being an entrepreneur is about endurance and patience. I've realized that everything takes time, success takes time, struggling through the low points takes time. Nothing is instant.

My biggest success as an entrepreneur remains getting my very first paying customer. What a rush; I still remember her name and seeing her transaction come through validated so much work and alleviated so much pressure.

The best advice I've received in my entrepreneurial journey is that my company is not more important than my family. If my wife is not a hundred percent on board with what I'm doing day in and day out, not only will my family suffer but the business will suffer as well. And so I make sure to prioritize time with my wife and make sure that she feels cared for, validated and appreciated as I'm on this journey, in this struggle to create and launch a successful company.

"I FINALLY LAUNCHED A SUCCESSFUL COMPANY AND I WAKE UP MOST NIGHTS, BECAUSE I STILL HAVE NO SALARY AND A BABY ON THE WAY."

CAROLINE
JOY

PRESIDENT
Caroline Joy Communications

"I AM TEACHING & PRESENTING AS AN EXPERT AND EVERY MORNING I WAKE UP WITH A PIT IN MY STOMACH WONDERING HOW AM I GOING TO PAY MY BILLS."

LYNN CLARK PORTRAITS

"WE HAVE BEEN EXCEEDING SALES GOALS AND I CAN BARELY MAKE RENT AND PAY OFF MY STUDENT LOANS."

Hello, I'm Cat Cook, the Art Director of Fourth Wall Productions. I grew up overseas, so every three years we would move to a different country. I was always an artist; I was continuously inspired by what was around me. And when I was in middle school, I made friends with a girl named Kiersty. She and I couldn't have been more different. She was someone who definitely kept to herself; I was and in your face. But she and I shared something in common. We love to design worlds and characters and just come up with endless ideas. One day she and I realized that we'd grow up and end up working for somebody, and it meant we'd never end up doing any of this again. So, she and I said, "Why don't we just create our own company? Yeah, let's be entrepreneurs."

We called it Nut House Productions because we're both super nutty. By the end of our high-school careers we chose the same college. We studied; we worked with the goal of our company in mind.

By the end of our college careers, we decided to make it happen. Well, it was very hard to get off the ground because it was only the two of us. We had no clue about how to start a business. She and I were both artists, and we ended up getting jobs. She went to Dairy Queen, I went to Starbucks. How were we supposed to start a company when we have to pay rent and have to pay off insane student loans? It just wasn't possible.

So, long story short, we went on our own separate adventures and she joined a startup game company the same time I joined a startup film company. When I joined Fourth Wall Productions, it was stressful. Every person in that company was working a second job. At that time, I was not only trying to be an entrepreneur of the business, but I was also working in daycare just to pay the bills.

I was so stressed out, but I thought, "Oh my God, this is my second chance. The first time didn't work out, but I'm going to make the second time work out. I don't care how rough it gets. I'm going to make it work."

It was so hard and stressful and no one had a life. And just when it had reached its worst, just when we all thought the company was going to fail and we were making other plans, it came through. Within a month's time, the entire situation flipped and instead of thinking, "Oh God, this is it, this is the last day, this company isn't going to possibly survive," it was on its feet again. And I can tell you it's still very stressful but it's worth it.

The biggest challenge you will face as an entrepreneur is that you will be stressed out of your gourd. I can't tell you that enough. Some people are just super cool, collected and very robotic, and good for them, they're so awesome. I'm not one of those people. There have been times when we're working at a billion things at once. And you can see the stress in every single person's face. And you get to a point where you realize, "I can't really do the things I really like doing, but I can't give this company up. There's no way, I'm not going to let it fail."

So my advice to you is please devote some time for yourself, no matter how many phone calls, no matter how many emails. Just take some time just for yourself to decompress every day, no matter what.

The biggest success of being an entrepreneur is the people. Straight up. I work with some of the nicest, most wonderful people on this planet. I am so lucky and remember that crowning moment when I was sitting at my desk and I looked over to my left and thought, "Oh man, she is so awesome." And I look over to my right. "Man, he is awesome. Everyone is awesome."

And nothing is more rewarding than after conquering a storm, going out to a brewery and sitting at a table with all my co-workers, my friends. We know everyone has sacrificed something and everyone acknowledges that: "We're alive! We've gone this far, we're not giving up, and you guys are amazing."

That connection to me is so worth it, when you can choose who you work with, who you share the struggle with. I always compare it to a crew on some kind of Navy ship and we're in the middle of a storm and it's super crazy. Then the storm passes and calm comes and we've made it. By the way, storms always happen, but every storm gets a little bit easier as you go down the road.

The best advice that I've ever received was from myself. I reached a point in my life where I could not be afraid of anything. You know what? Being scared just disables you from making any progress in your life. If you are too scared to put yourself out there, take risks, take chances, you can't get anywhere. I realized that at a point of my life where I was suffering from depression.

If you know me I'm a very talkative, extroverted person and I love hiking and adventuring and I'm so passionate. It's hard to imagine me depressed. It happens. It can happen to anybody and I remember when I made the conscious decision: Don't give up. No matter how much hurt you receive, no matter how many blisters and bruises and scratches you receive, you will get up and you're going to make the most out of your life and I did. Be a badass no matter who you are, what you look like, where you're from. If you want to be happy, be your own badass.

"I WAS OUT OF WORK, IN DEBT, AND IN A LOT OF PHYSICAL PAIN FROM A BACK INJURY, AND ALL THE PEOPLE IN MY LIFE BELIEVED IN MY POTENTIAL TO BECOME WHAT I AM TODAY."

My name is Clay Cousins and my company is called Elevate Momentum. We do executive coaching, large-scale multi-stakeholder group facilitation, and strategic HR advisory work.

Why did I want to become an entrepreneur? Throughout my life I have always had ideas and schemes. And most people that I was close to said that I was an entrepreneur. It took me the first half of my life to really embrace that concept and accept it as true. And now I love the flexibility of discovering new problems and setting my own schedule and being able to move between industries with our work, which in a traditional business wouldn't be possible.

The biggest challenge is feeling comfortable that we're moving in the right direction and having faith that it's all going to work out, especially when we were first starting the business. Once you get it off the ground and running and get some validation it becomes much easier, but having that initial faith that your idea is a good idea and that there's a market for it was probably the biggest challenge for us.

The biggest success would be picking my business partner, who is actually my wife. It has been rewarding to define the business that we wanted to start and work together, use each other's skills, and have conversations where we're able to meet the needs of each other from all aspects of life. Especially in the business sense that we're working towards a larger goal than either she or I could accomplish by ourselves.

The best advice that I ever received as an entrepreneur was from a family friend of ours who said, "Always work yourself out of a job." The meaning to me is that if you're finding your replacement and working yourself out of a job, it opens up opportunity for you to move into.

I've shared that with many people and they look at me like I'm a little crazy. The meaning behind it is about creating opportunity for someone to replace you so that then you can move into the next opportunities for yourself and continue to grow within your career.

DANIELLE
NORRIS

CO-FOUNDER
+ CEO
sovenco

I'm Danielle Norris, the Co-Founder and CEO of Sovenco, which stands for Social Venture Company. We provide management consulting services through our virtual platform and a unique business framework for growth companies that have set out to solve BIG social and environmental issues that plague our world.

I realized entrepreneurship was my chosen career path at the age of eighteen. At that moment in my life, I was overcoming severe childhood challenges while raising my two-year-old daughter, attending school, and working a job that paid enough to support my family as a young single mother. The ability to work a traditional 9-to-5 job was and still is impossible with kids. I still joke with friends and family that I was on an attendance write-up for the entire nine years of my corporate career from missing work for kid issues. This issue was magnified when I pursued a career in real estate and consulting. My dream to change the world through innovation of management consulting was not going to happen for me in the traditional way.

My biggest challenge as an entrepreneur is not being able to predict the unknown. No matter how many spreadsheets I create, market research I complete, and powerful mentors who support me, I have to lean-in to the extreme lows (and highs) of entrepreneurship. Other challenges are having to manage "the dips," as Seth Godin says, while having the pressure of being constantly in the public eye when would I rather be the geek behind the scenes.

My biggest success has been seeing my vision come to fruition. Not only in market tractions, but in the impact created from my business. It is magical to cry with clients and those they serve, not just from struggles but from the joy of seeing their companies create social or environmental impact. To see a plan we supported become law, like a piece of legislation that supports ending human trafficking. We got to help make that happen. To be there when lives are saved and new pathways of hope are formed is an amazing feeling every time.

"I FEAR DAILY WHEN I HAVE TO STAND AT THE FRONT OF THE ROOM AND I'D RATHER BE HIDDEN IN THE BACK AND MY LIFE'S PURPOSE IS FULLY ALIGNED WITH MY BUSINESS."

DANIELLE
NORRIS

The best advice I have received as an entrepreneur was from one of my first mentors. He said, "You don't always have to stick to the plan, Danielle." And to this day that has made a huge difference in my life, because as an entrepreneur you cannot always stick to the plan; you're going to have to pivot.

The advice I would give to newbie entrepreneurs is that you need to know yourself. Before you even start, you have to have a reality check on who you are, your strengths, weaknesses, and abilities. Who do you have to support you? Do you have an influential network? Do you thrive in challenging situations? Have you chosen a supportive life partner? Do you have financial support? You will still need to be open to growth, as you will leap forward in your journey, but there will be years of pre-work before you start-up.

Timing, perseverance, and ten years of trying will eventually make you look like an overnight success.
- *Biz Stone, co-founder Twitter*

"I ENDED UP IN THE HOSPITAL FROM STRESS AND EXHAUSTION AND THAT WAS THE CATALYST FOR UNDERSTANDING THAT MY PHYSICAL AND MENTAL WELL BEING ARE CRITICAL TO RUNNING A SUCCESSFUL BUSINESS."

I'm the CEO of Technical Integrity, the business that I have been running now for more than seven years. The focus is on professional placement and team-building for engineering, sales, and executive staff for startups in Colorado. We love what we do. We have a very large community-first and give-first mission.

I would say I became an entrepreneur out of necessity. After 10 years of being an employee in the staffing realm, I was really unhappy with the model that existed then. The attitude was there was no reason to pay attention to culture or fit. Everything had to do with getting a bunch of "seats" and doing that as quickly as possible without regard to the aspirations of the people that we were helping to find jobs. On the other side, the employers were very large organizations who admitted that they were going to send the business offshore within six months, and they were working with 30 different vendors. I believed this was a broken model and I fell in love with the Boulder startup community. I knew that they needed a partner to help find the best talent, and we set out to do the right thing.

We knew there were a lot of others in the recruiting realm and we wanted to become trusted advisors; we set out to be partners. I fell in love with the idea of the of "give first" ethos while sitting in the New Tech Meetups, listening to Robert Reich, David Cohen and Brad Feld, who has since become a mentor. I understood that there were real ways that we could give back to the community. We would build trust by putting together important events like Ignite Boulder, Boulder/Denver New Tech Meetup, and Startup Weekend.

All of that lead to the ability to share our stories, just like we are doing here. We love what Denver and Boulder are all about and being a trusted advisor in the recruiting realm. When people in Techstars, Foundry Group, and Access Venture Partners have openings, they come to us and we feel really good about that.

The biggest success is that we are now completely embraced by the startup community and we are a critical component to putting on the Denver/ Boulder Startup Week and all of the other important events. We love to be enmeshed in the community.

 The best advice is from my father. He told me that the only thing you really own in your life is your integrity. I didn't really understand what that meant for a long time, but I've come to understand that through the years people really respond to how you conduct yourself every day, all day. If you are completely forthright and own your mistakes and just act in the best interest of the community, you know you are acting with integrity. So that is where Technical Integrity's name comes from.

My advice to entrepreneurs is to listen to your gut. My philosophy is that there is something in you, whether it's in your brain or your gut, your consciousness is telling you something is wrong if it's wrong and right if it's right. And if you are doing something your gut is telling you is good, bad, or indifferent, then it's time to listen because it is never wrong. In my experience, listen to your gut if there's something that you love and you know you have a passion for it, then follow it and the money will come later. Just listen to your gut. Don't ever drown that out. It's the best advice I can give.

Success is how high you bounce after you hit bottom.

– General George Patton

Hi, my name is Gerald Barton, the founder of a business called SFH Bookkeeping and Financial Services.

From a young age, I knew I wanted to be an entrepreneur, but like many others I followed the path of education and went to college, and then spent the first 11 years of my career in corporate America. I was always good at what I did, but I was never really fulfilled. So in 2005, I finally became an entrepreneur to find fulfillment in truly serving other people and to get the freedom and flexibility of my time.

The biggest challenge in being an entrepreneur is not knowing what's next. Is next month going to be a good month or a bad month? Will there be client challenges, will everything go smoothly next month? Are our clients getting what they need from us or do they need more? Do we even know what else they need? So just not knowing is our biggest challenge.

Our biggest success is having a business that serves both my staff and our clients, and the culture that comes with that. When I send a paycheck to a staff person or make a deposit into their retirement account, it feels really good. That's a win. That's a success. My little business is contributing in a positive way to the financial well-being of their family. And when we give relief to a client when we've solved a problem, that's a win, that's a success. And so just the culture that comes with serving people both internally and externally, I would say that definitely is our biggest success.

I received a lot of great advice along the way from a lot of amazing people, but the very best advice that I ever received is: In everything you do, whether it's in your personal life or your business life, it must be congruent with your "big why." If your "big why" isn't the foundation of everything you do, there's just going to always be this internal conflict, this inconsistency in the way you're handling yourself during the course of a day.

"I LOST A BUSINESS TO BANKRUPTCY, SWALLOWED MY PRIDE, AND BOUNCED BACK WITH A NEW BUSINESS MODEL TO HELP REAL ESTATE INVESTORS AVOID THE SAME TRAPS THAT HAD FORCED MY PRIOR BUSINESS INTO BANKRUPTCY."

"WE'RE GOING THROUGH A CHALLENGE WHERE WE EXPERIENCE CONTINUOUS GROWTH AND FEEL STUCK AS IF GROWTH IS NON-EXISTENT."

HECTOR
SIMOUDIS

**CHIEF
STORYTELLER
+ LEGACY
OFFICER**

vp legacies

My name is Hector Simoudis, one of the co-owners of VP Legacies LLC, and my title is Chief Storyteller and Legacy Officer. Entrepreneurship has always been in my blood, and I discovered at a young age that I wanted to become an entrepreneur. I've had the beautiful experience of not only growing up in the Middle East and also being 100 percent Greek, but more importantly, traveling to all corners of the world. I've been to over 30 countries and really experienced entrepreneurship at its core. I truly fell in love with it and knew that entrepreneurship, being with people, inspiring people, helping people take their dream and make it a reality is something that I always wanted to do. It dates back to being 13 years old and starting an American candy shop in the Middle East. At 15 years old I moved to the United States and started bringing Middle Eastern products over here as well.

One of my biggest challenges as an entrepreneur was first getting started; I was all over the place. I didn't know what to do. I was struggling and I learned, and this led into one of my biggest successes, which is focusing on mentorship and guidance. Look for people who are willing to help, who you want to be a part of your journey. If it wasn't for those people, I wouldn't be here today. I'm very fortunate that I've had a lot of mentorship and advisors to help bring me to where I am today.

And some of the best advice I ever received is:
Know what you're doing. In other words, know your why. Why do you do what you do? Why have you created your business, and most importantly, why are you doing what you're doing to impact your customers? Both of my mentors said that if you can't see your value proposition, if you can't see your strategy, most importantly if you don't know your why and the impact that you're causing, you're going to tumble. And that's something I've embraced since day one.

As an entrepreneur, you always experience ups and you always experience downs. But that's the beautiful piece about entrepreneurship. It's really embracing those up and down moments. But more importantly, not just focusing on the positive, but focusing on the times when things are challenging, the times when things are tough. And really embracing and loving those moments.

It is impossible to live without failing at something, unless you live so cautiously that you might as well not have lived at all, in which case you have failed by default.

- J.K. Rowling

"I CLOSED DOWN MY FIRST TWO BUSINESSES AND AM FINALLY FINDING SUCCESS WITH MY THIRD BUSINESS."

My name is Helene Kwong and I am the CEO and Co-founder of Hashtagitude. I became an entrepreneur because I wanted to definitely make an impact on the world and I felt that with my first business, which was helping foreign nationals find internships or full-time work in the United States, I could make a bigger impact versus working for an employer at a company. I do enjoy the flexibility of entrepreneurship and I do enjoy working with the kind of clients I have so far with Hashtagitude.

My biggest challenge with being an entrepreneur has been growing businesses versus just starting them and stopping them. I have two previous businesses that I shut down, primarily because I wasn't making much money with them and I didn't feel like they were my true passion. I was very sad actually with my first business when I shut it down, but now I feel that was the best decision to make.

My biggest success so far has been growing and sustaining Hashtagitude and knowing how to invest better back into the business. With my first two businesses, I didn't know what kind of services or investments to make for the business and I thought I needed all these special things that I didn't actually need. So now I'm a little wary but also a lot smarter about what to invest in for the business, such as: Do I need office space or can I work at a co-working space? Do I need to pay for an email service or can I go with a free one? Making more educated decisions has been the biggest success and that's helped me sustain Hashtagitude.

There are two pieces of really good advice I have received in my journey. The first one is from my business coach last year. She instructed me on how I need to invest in myself and in my business before I can attract the kind of clients I want. I know that I struggle with feeling "good enough," but I also struggle with trying to find clients who know they need my services.

Last year I was struggling with a feeling of scarcity. It turns out that I was manifesting that scarcity response in my prospects, so they didn't feel like they could afford to work with Hashtagitude.

And once I worked on this with my business coach, I have more clarity and I felt a lot more confident about offering my services to new prospects.

The second piece of advice that has been integral though my whole life is from my dad: If anything comes up, no problem. My dad is an immigrant; he came from mainland China to the U.S. He hardly knew any English, and learned it through the people he has met. He owned his restaurant for 30 years. His motto or mantra is: "It's no problem. Nothing is too hard, and any new challenge is a new opportunity to learn."

Your value doesn't decrease based on someone's inability to see your worth.

- Ted Rubin

HOLLY
LEVINGSTON

CO-FOUNDER, CEO
Surgical Alternatives

"I WAS OFFERED THE OPPORTUNITY OF A LIFETIME TO BE CEO OF A SUCCESSFUL COMPANY AND IN TURN, DISSOLVED THE COMPANY I LAUNCHED A YEAR AGO."

"I AM THE FIRST PERSON IN MY GROUP OF FRIENDS OR FAMILY TO BUILD A BUSINESS AND IT HAS CREATED A RIFT IN MY PERSONAL RELATIONSHIPS."

JACQUELINE
ROS

My name is Jacqueline Ros and I became an entrepreneur because people hurt my little sister and I wanted to be able to protect her. My company is called Revolar, and we make wearable safety devices that help keep your loved ones safe.

My biggest challenge as an entrepreneur is knowing when the right decision is for you to continue to grow with the business or figure out what you want your role to be as you begin to specialize. I hired a new CEO because I realized I wanted to play to my strengths and learn at a more reasonable pace.

Our biggest success has been the people we've helped. It's really amazing to see how we've made an impact on these people's lives.

The best advice I've ever received is that bad news travels fast, and as an entrepreneur you're always getting bad news. Share it fast, and you can start to get help. The advice I'd give other entrepreneurs is: don't ever feel stuck, you have the right to grow your business however it feels good for you. Don't feel like you have to become something you're not or feel pressure to continue do that in order to grow.

JEFFERY
REEVES

FOUNDER, CEO, FORCE COMMANDER
Profit Pilots, Inc.

"I OWN A DISRUPTIVE COMPANY THAT
COULD PRODUCE $100MM+ REVENUE
BY 2020 AND LACK THE RESOURCES
TO SCALE IT RAPIDLY ENOUGH TO
MAKE THAT HAPPEN."

JOHN
SCHNIPKOWEIT

CEO | FOUNDER
NextStep.io

"WE ARE CLOSING A SIX FIGURE
CONTRACT AND I FEEL LIKE
ITS NOT ENOUGH TO KEEP
MY HEAD ABOVE WATER."

JOSHUA
WHITAKER

CEO
Denver Custom Websites

"I MOVED TO COLORADO WITH THE AMERICAN DREAM, LOST IT ALL IN ONE WEEK, AND NOW I HAVE IT ALL AGAIN."

"THIS YEAR I LEFT MY JOB TO BUILD MY OWN BUSINESS AND I UNDERESTIMATED WHAT IT WOULD TAKE TO DO THAT WHILE PREGNANT WITH A NEW BABY."

KATHRYN
ROMAN

Hi, my name is Kathryn Roman and I'm the Founder of Denver Natural Mom. I became an entrepreneur because I realized that I could. I come from a family of small business owners and I'm married to an entrepreneur, and for a long time I thought that I wasn't cut out for that life. When I started facing some dissatisfaction with working for other people, it was a process of building the confidence to realize that I could do this too, and I could work for myself and create something from scratch that didn't exist before.

For me the biggest challenge of being an entrepreneur is definitely the part of the job that doesn't end. You know, when 5:00 p.m. comes around and you don't clock out. It bleeds into home and personal life and family and I'm a mom of two. In fact my youngest is only four weeks old. So my biggest challenge is the juggling act and managing my own expectations for myself and for my business.

My biggest success has certainly been creating something and being recognized in my industry for what my website contributes to this community, this physical community of Denver. And I am booked for my first speaking gig next month and it's just such a recognition that the community wants and is interested in what I have to say and what we offer.

The best advice I ever received was to accept each day, that the day had happened exactly the way it was supposed to. This has been so reinforcing for me, to believe that God's looking out for me and my family life and my home life with my business. And to not beat myself up for something that didn't go the way I thought it would or because I underperformed. It takes the pressure off and it keeps me feeling productive and positive even if I'm down, to know that today is not what I expected, but it happened exactly the way it was supposed to. That person that I met, that person that blew me off, that was exactly what was supposed to happen. And that's just one of the ways that I trick myself into looking forward and moving forward even when it feels like I have no momentum to do that.

"I SIGNED A $4M DEAL, OUR LARGEST EVER, AND ALL I CAN THINK ABOUT IS WHEN WE'RE GOING TO RUN OUT OF MONEY."

KRISTA
MORGAN

**CO-FOUNDER
+ CEO**
p2binvestor

I'm Krista Morgan, the CEO and Co-Founder of P2Binvestor. We are a marketplace lender and we offer fast, flexible and affordable working capital to good businesses with big ambitions. I became an entrepreneur because there was a point in my career when I realized I didn't like the options in front of me. I was living in London, working at a large digital marketing agency. The company had so many women in all disciplines of the business, but only one woman on the leadership team. And I learned pretty quickly that whenever I worked really hard I would get more responsibility. I would get no increase in pay and my boss would get promoted. So given those options, the decision to move to a new country and start a new life and a new business that I was passionate about was actually a very simple one to make.

I would say one of our biggest challenges right now is figuring out how to maintain our company culture as we grow. As our team grows and we add a lot of moving parts, there are different dynamics, which make it hard to maintain the feeling that we're all operating as one cohesive unit.

Suddenly we were at the 25-person mark and started to see silos. So we're scheduling more all-hands meetings and more time for the team to relax and build personal relationships with one another.

We started waffle Wednesdays, which I think is pretty awesome. I am extremely proud of the growth that we have accomplished. In the past year we've grown our team to over 30 people, we've moved into a new, very cool office that makes us look more like a real tech company, and we've been named one of the fastest-growing businesses in Denver, based on our revenue growth. I'm also very proud that we've figured out our niche in the market and our entire team is focused on executing on our vision.

Some of the best advice I ever received — which I'll admit I didn't listen to early on — was to focus on understanding our customers and getting to cash-flow positive before anything else. We raised and spent a million dollars before we found a single customer. I was so focused on finding investors and building the infrastructure we would need when the floodgates opened and customers came pouring in that I forgot to find the customers. If I were doing it all over again I would absolutely focus on understanding "Who is my customer? How do I sell to them, how do I find them?" I would spend money on that and only that and then raise money to focus on scaling the rest of the business.

My best advice for other entrepreneurs, especially first-time entrepreneurs like myself, is to ask yourself what expertise you're missing around the table and go find someone to fill that void. The biggest thing I've learned over the past few years of running this business is that I make significantly better decisions when I'm surrounded by people who are a lot smarter than I am, who have real domain expertise that I don't have. I absolutely believe it will have an incredible impact on your growth trajectory if you make those key hires earlier than you think you need to.

Biggest mistake you can make is listening to people who've given up on their dreams telling you to give up on yours.

- *Umair Hague*

KRYSTAL
COVINGTON

I'm Krystal Covington and I'm CEO and founder of Women of Denver, a Social Enterprise Association for women. I became an entrepreneur simply because I had personally found a need and I didn't see anyone filling that need in the way that I wanted to experience it. I needed a network for myself, and the networking groups I was going to were mostly focused on sales and not on collaboration and long-term relationships that I wanted to build.

I'd say my biggest challenge has been educating customers when there's so many other competing programs. It takes some education to teach potential customers why what we do is different. We're not like everybody else, but my success is relying on other people understanding that, on being educated about what the differences are.

Our biggest success as a business has been building a profitable business from scratch and keeping the momentum the last couple of years. We're currently getting bigger each quarter, so the growth is definitely exponential.

The best advice I've ever received is to stop making things about me. I was afraid to sell in the beginning because I felt really uncomfortable asking people to spend money. When I learned is that by not selling the program, I was potentially keeping people from a resource they really needed. People needed Women of Denver, but in my head it was just, "I'm selling something and it's uncomfortable."

 So now I realize that being fearful of selling is my selfishness, so I need to make sure that I'm sharing what I'm doing with other women so that they know that this is available as an option for them. If I needed it, they need it too.

"I HAD A SUCCESFUL LAUNCH AND I'M SUFFERING FROM ANXIETY ABOUT THE RESPONSIBILITY OF IT ALL."

The advice that I would give is to stay focused and don't let yourself be distracted by other people who mimic what you are doing. I've seen a lot of copycat programs come along, and they have pulled my customers away for a time because they were shiny and new. But in the end, they all closed up. They close up shop because they don't have a core vision like the Women of Denver has. So yes, there will be competitors, but if you just focus on what you do well and do it the best that you can, people will be attracted to that, they will be motivated by that, and they will be loyal to that. So keep doing what you're doing and be passionate about it.

Let's get real.
Tell your story.
Impactfounder.com

CO-FOUNDER
+ CHIEF
BUSINESS
DEVELOPMENT
OFFICER
sovenco

My name is Laura Franklin and I am the Co-founder and Chief Business Development Officer of Sovenco. During college I met my business partner; we were in a few classes together. We both had this massive feeling of disillusionment about how businesses were being run in the United States. We graduated during the Great Recession, which was brought on by corporate greed. It made me want to try running my own business and I became an entrepreneur to create something for myself rather than working in a corporate job.

As an entrepreneur my biggest challenge is making enough money. My husband just moved to the US, and as his chief sponsor for getting a green card, I have to prove to the government that I'm making enough to support him, which I'm not, because I'm an entrepreneur.

My biggest success as a business, 100% it's been the first few sales that my business partner and I got. It felt so powerful to realize that what we're selling not only had value, but people would pay thousands of dollars for it. I felt like I was just walking on air after we got those first few sales. It's the best feeling in the world.

The best advice I've ever received as an entrepreneur is from my business partner Danielle: Just never give up. I come from a really rigid family; you're supposed to just get a job. So as an entrepreneur it's been difficult for me to reconcile myself, coming from that environment. But my business partner is always there to tell me to never give up and that's powerful.

"MY BUSINESS IS GROWING FASTER THAN I EVER COULD HAVE EXPECTED AND I HAVE CONSTANT STOMACH PAIN FROM THE STRESS OF IT ALL."

"I FOLLOWED MY DREAMS TO BECOME AN ENTREPRENEUR, THE MOST FULFILLING THING I'VE DONE IN MY LIFE, AND I OFTEN FEEL ALONE AND MISUNDERSTOOD. "

LAWRENCE
WAGNER

CEO +
FOUNDER
spark mindset

Hi, my name is Lawrence Wagner, I'm the CEO and Founder of Spark Mindset. Why did I become an entrepreneur? I became an entrepreneur to empower people to follow their dreams and pursue the things that they're passionate about and to develop their purpose.

At my old job I felt trapped, I felt like I couldn't do these things, I felt like I couldn't explore. So, I decided that I wanted more out of my life than a six-figure paycheck. I decided that empowering people and helping people gave me meaning, fulfillment and purpose, and I love what I do.

What is my biggest challenge? I think my biggest challenge is the lack of support from the community that I've poured so much into. It was difficult when I reached out to so many people for help and they turned me away. They either didn't have time, or all of a sudden didn't have the resources. I had poured so much of myself into a community that did not in return pour back to me. So I felt alone, I felt depressed. There were times that I wanted to quit, I felt misunderstood. My biggest challenge is that I felt like I wasn't valuable because these people didn't help me and they didn't come alongside of me like they said they would.

My biggest success is the team I have developed around me. They help get the word out, we push each other, there are people I can go along this journey with and so I no longer feel alone and they help me understand that I had a powerful statement and a powerful movement.

The best advice I've ever received is: The grind never stops. And that means that I'm an entrepreneur 24 hours a day. I'm always thinking, I'm always writing things down, I'm always checking things. It doesn't mean I don't spend time with friends and family, doesn't mean that I don't take a minute to pause. But this business is a part of who I am and its success depends on me.

LIDIANE
MOCKO

OWNER
mocko
consulting

My name is Lidiane Mocko and I am the owner of Mocko Consulting Small Business CRM Solutions. I became an entrepreneur because I was tired of trying to fit into roles working for other people and other companies. And I felt like it was time for me to do something on my own. So I did.

My biggest challenge was to get my message across and explain to people what I do with Mocko Consulting. And the biggest success is persisting in trying to address that challenge. I started doing one blog post a month and one newsletter a month, and now I can see the response. Right after I send a newsletter, people are contacting me for new opportunities.

The best advice I have received is to persist; you know business is about not giving up, learning from whatever challenge you face and moving on to the next, and that's how you go.

And here is something I wrote about my work with my best friend from college. It's on the "about us" page of our new brand called Mocknick apps. So it's a tale of longtime friends:

"Simone and Lidiane were born in the same year and in the same state. Simone was born and raised inland, Lidiane grew up on the coast. Simone is blonde and Lidiane is brunette. They are far away and very close. Simone is in Brazil, Lidiane is in the US. When they were teenagers they both moved to Florianopolis, they met at the University of Santa Catarina. They were both part of the computer science class. They are similar and different at the same time. Lidiane was always out and about, Simone liked peace and quiet. They took classes together, worked hard together, traveled together and sometimes went to parties together. Simone graduated first, Lidiane right after. After graduation, they had entrepreneurial aspirations. But life got in the way. Simone became a Master of knowledge engineering; Lidiane immigrated to the US and got an MBA. Now the time is right and the business opportunity is bright."

The best advice I have received is to persist, to not give up, learn from the challenges and move on.

"MY BUSINESS PARTNER DECIDED
TO LEAVE AND OPENED
SPACE FOR ANOTHER PERSON
TO JOIN ME IN MY BUSINESS!"

"I'VE DEDICATED MY ENTIRE LIFE HELPING PEOPLE REACH THEIR HIGHEST POTENTIAL AND I CONSTANTLY WORRY THAT I WILL NEVER REACH MINE."

FOUNDER
the leadership
influence

My name is Lori Heisler and I'm the Founder of The Leadership Influence. I became an entrepreneur because I was working as an educator in a system that cared more about test scores than it did about people. I firmly believe in being the change you wish to see in the world and I wanted to empower people, to know that they matter. My biggest challenge as an entrepreneur is trusting and knowing that I'm good enough. It gets in the way of taking consistent action and showing up for myself and others.

My biggest success is staying true to my values and modeling the way for others so that they can do the same. The best advice I ever received is that your greatest gift is your greatest challenge.

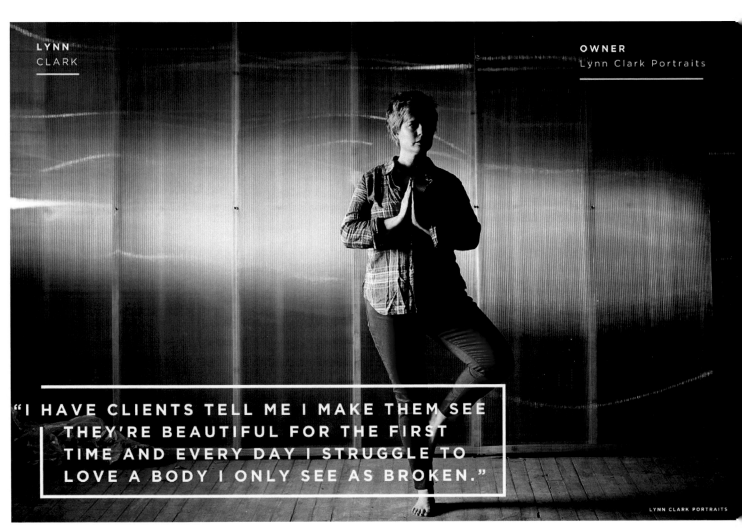

LYNN
CLARK

OWNER
Lynn Clark Portraits

"I HAVE CLIENTS TELL ME I MAKE THEM SEE
THEY'RE BEAUTIFUL FOR THE FIRST
TIME AND EVERY DAY I STRUGGLE TO
LOVE A BODY I ONLY SEE AS BROKEN."

LYNN CLARK PORTRAITS

MANDY STRAIGHT

INTERIOR DESIGNER

mandy
straight, inc

Hi my name is Mandy Straight, my business is Mandy Straight Inc. My title is Interior Designer, based around the statement "Design a life you love and live in it."

Why did I become an entrepreneur? I became an entrepreneur by accident. I moved to a new city. I didn't like the prospects that were there for job opportunities and I thought, "I've been doing this design thing for a while, about 10 years, and I know how to help people with what they need for design. I can do this on my own."

So now I'm a little bit addicted to the schedule and I'm definitely addicted to being able to help my clients in the best way for them, not the way my company tells me I have to.

What is my biggest challenge as an entrepreneur? My biggest challenge is seeing the big picture and knowing what I'm working toward. Secondary to that would be how to break it down. I'm really good at putting in the work and the enthusiasm that it takes to get things done. I just get a little lost in the trees and I need some help seeing the clarity and my own purpose.

What is my biggest success? That is, hands down, giving a TED Talk. My TED Talk moment was just unbelievable. It was a life bucket-list moment, and speaking in front of thousands of people, sharing a message that I think can make them happier and make their lives better was just unbeatable. That's by far the best moment.

For the best advice I've ever received, I'm going to give a quote by Elizabeth Gilbert. It's in her book Big Magic. She says to do whatever brings you to life, then follow your own fascinations, obsessions and compulsions, trust them, and create whatever causes a revolution in your heart.

I think it's so true that what causes a revolution in our hearts can also cause that in others, and I think it's so important that we share it. The other piece of advice that I think is just vital to being an entrepreneur is that you're never ready. I tend to be a perfectionist, and that means that I don't like starting until I know all of the variables, which means that I don't always get started. So, I am getting a crash course in not being ready and acting in spite of that.

"I GAVE A TED TALK AND I STILL STRUGGLE WITH FEELING LIKE I DON'T HAVE ENOUGH TO OFFER CLIENTS."

84

MARGO
ELFSTROM

FOUNDER
Margo Elfstrom Photography

"I AM DOING THE MOST VOLUME THAT I EVER
HAVE AND I STRUGGLE WITH ACCEPTING
THAT I'M ALLOWED TO BE SUCCESSFUL."

LYNN CLARK PORTRAITS

"I SOLD MY REAL ESTATE COMPANY TO INVEST IN MY NEXT STARTUP AND WE'RE STILL NOT MAKING A PROFIT 2 YEARS IN."

My name is Matt Holmes and I'm the Founder of Handshakin. I became an entrepreneur early on, while still in college, because of all the same reasons everyone else does: the flexible schedule, the retiring at 35, the sexiness of it. But not today. It's something much bigger than all that for me. But that's what got me interested in it with my first company.

The biggest challenge I'm facing and I've ever faced is how to get more work done when you don't have the resources to pay people full-time. I think that's a pretty common challenge for entrepreneurs.

The biggest success I had was when I sold off and got out of real estate. After years of grinding and hustling and not getting paid, I was able to actually have a six-digit paycheck. Not anything like a tech startup exit, but I got a break, I got a huge paycheck.

And with my current company, Handshakin, we have a video series where we interviewed top entrepreneurs. And the best advice I ever received is from one of the billionaires that was on the show, John Paul DeJoria. He told me that you have to pay it forward and give first right away. The example he used is when you're going down the highway and you see that car broken down on the side of the road, you actually have to make the decision right there on the spot to pull over and help them. If you passed that car and say you'll do it next time, that's not how you're going to reach entrepreneurial success. You're going to achieve entrepreneurial success by paying it forward and helping others, because a network of people that you've helped out and that want to give you a favor genuinely is the only way to grow a startup when you are bootstrapping and don't have funding to hire a huge team.

MATT
MILLER

PRESIDENT
Base Performance

"I LOVE THAT WHAT I DO HELPS
PEOPLE LIVE HEALTHIER LIVES,
AND I LIVE IN A CONSTANT
STATE OF PARANOIA THAT I
MIGHT HAVE TO REPEAT THE
LESSONS OF LIFE THAT I HAVE
FAILED TO LEARN."

MICHELLE
ARCHULETA

My name is Michelle Archuleta and I'm the Founder and visionary of my company, Doctor Speak. I became an entrepreneur because I am inspired by my grandmother. She was diagnosed with colon cancer when I was in college, which led me to a career in cancer research. I worked at the Broad Institute of MIT at Harvard. I then went on and worked at a pharmaceutical company where I helped make decisions to take drugs into the clinic. This work was very exciting, however when I thought back on my grandmother, it really wasn't a drug or a biomarker that I was looking for. It was knowledge, it was her feeling comfortable asking her doctor, "Should I have a colonoscopy?" So it was much more about knowledge and empowering patients and giving them an opportunity to get the best health care out there. And so, this led to my company, Doctor Speak.

The biggest challenge is that I'm the sole source of income for my family. My biggest success is seeing people use our product and seeing that light bulb go off in their heads and seeing that "aha" moment. Now they feel comfortable, now they feel like they can ask a question, now they feel like they can be engaged.

The best advice that I've received is that if you truly want to do something, if you really want to change, make a small commitment to it every day. You'd be amazed at how just a little bit of time everyday can turn into a beautiful dream come true.

"MY COMPANY CAN MAKE A DIFFERENCE IN SO MANY PEOPLE'S LIVES AND MY FAMILY RELIES ON ME FOR THE SOLE SOURCE OF INCOME."

"MY SALES ARE DOUBLING EACH MONTH AND I WAKE UP AT 2 EVERY MORNING WITH ANXIETY ATTACKS."

CEO +
CO-FOUNDER
the carlin

Hi, my name is Mihoko Ward and my product is The Carlin. It's a patent-pending hair accessory I created to dramatically improve how women get ready in the morning. It is named Carlin after my dog. The Carlin means pug in French. I began my career at PricewaterhouseCoopers and worked in wealth management firms like Morgan Stanley. I spent fifteen years in corporate America as a CPA but I always knew I wanted to have my own business. I wanted to build something my own; something meaningful that can help people. But I promised my parents back in Japan that I would get a job after college because my father had a failed business experience. When I was in university, he had to file bankruptcy and so my parents have always asked me to get a good job at a great company and that's what I did.

But I wasn't very happy. So when I finally had an idea and was able to develop a product, I decided to leave the corporate job. I know my life would be much easier staying in the corporate world; I had a good salary, I had a great a job. But building business was what I wanted to do, so I had to listen to my heart. And I'm really happy for what I did, I'm really happy building my business even though it's very difficult.

As a solo entrepreneur, it can be a lonely journey. I'm planting seeds every day to grow my business. Sometimes I get lucky and seeds start to grow and those are great days, great moments. But some seeds don't go anywhere, some seeds die pretty quickly and I have to find another way or start over again.

I'm responsible to motivate myself, decide on direction and keep taking actions. I do experience a lot of self-doubt and anxiety on a daily basis, but I'm learning every day to keep making progress, and I remind myself to be patient.

The biggest challenge is that no matter how I feel in the moment, I must take steps towards my goals. Although I need to scale more, I'm happy with how many products I was able to sell since I launched my website in June 2016. So far I have had no returns and I received great feedback from my customers. It is wonderful to know that a product I created can actually help other people. I also met great people to learn from and work with in the process and I'm so grateful for that. I hired a videographer to create the official video. We start filming on Monday and I'm really excited about that.

The best advice I have heard is to follow your heart and trust that it knows where it's going. This is by Steve Jobs, he said this at a Stanford commencement speech and it always stuck with me. I'm a pretty logical person. I'm a CPA, so I look for data, analytics and logic, but I also know how important our intuition is and when I heard Steve Jobs said to trust your heart, it really sank in. When I'm panicking or having anxiety attacks or having those moments where I feel so lost, I get quiet and I try to listen to my heart, try to listen to what my inner voice is trying to tell me.

I have not failed. I've just found 10,000 ways that won't work.

- *Thomas A. Edison*

"I AM AT THE TOP OF MY GAME AND I CAME OUT OF THE CLOSET. "

'm Mike Biselli, and my company is Catalyst HTI. We bring together digital health startups and Fortune 20 companies to fix American healthcare.

Being an entrepreneur means this is not work, this is part of who I am, it's part of who we are as entrepreneurs. I think authentically living in everything that you do as an entrepreneur is very important. That came across to me when I jumped off the entrepreneurial cliff back in 2011. Before that I said I need to live authentically on a personal level and that's when I came out of the closet. I said "I can't continue to get people to authentically believe in me if I'm not even being authentic to myself." And so authenticity is running through everything that I do personally, professionally, with my relationships, friendships etc.

It unlocked my full potential. It was unbelievable. In my career, on paper, I always knew I was doing quite well. But I always had this facade, always had to think up the next white lie to keep my sexuality closeted. I was able to finally not have to devote energy to that and I could devote it to other things, to where it actually matters.

And to be honest with you I didn't lose a single friendship. It was the best thing I could have ever done for myself. Mentally, spiritually, for my mission in life, everything. Living authentically in everything you do is game changing.

We have to get more authentic, we have to get more real; this is not an easy game. People see the media and think "I am going to be the next Mark Zuckerberg, look, it's so easy. He's made billions of dollars." NO, it's not. Some people say, "Mike you have the sexiest job in the world, you're a startup founder, you get to make your own reality."

And I'm thinking, "You don't understand how hard this is." How hard it is on yourself, on your family members, the energy it takes. We have to get more real as founders with one another and more importantly get real and transparent for the next generation of founders to help empower them to continue to change our world. Because that's what founders and entrepreneurs do: they change the world. We have two generations of founders who have already taken the plunge. Help encourage the next generation to be open, transparent, and be real. It's very healthy.

I jumped on the Impact Founder project early because I saw the clear value of what this will do for communities across the globe.

It's creating an opportunity to get real with one another. One big aspect for Catalyst is to reimagine healthcare from a mental health and behavioral approach. I tell people, "Why can I go to a happy hour with you and say 'I just had the most killer arm exercise at the gym.' Why can't I go to that same happy hour with you guys and say, 'I just had the most incredible hour with my therapist?'" Why is that a stigma in our culture? That's one thing that keeps me very passionate about what we're doing with Catalyst in my leadership position in healthcare. We need to demystify all of that, and I think Impact Founder is doing that as well. We need to get real. Practicing vulnerability actually opens up more doors. It opens up more opportunity.

Vulnerability is the birthplace of innovation.

- Brené Brown

"A LOT OF PEOPLE BELIEVE IN ME AND KNOW THAT I'M GOING TO BE A SUCCESSFUL ENTREPRENEUR AND I OFTEN FEEL LIKE A TOTAL FRAUD."

I'm Mike Kilcoyne the Founder of Embrace the Suck. I became an entrepreneur because I would be remiss to not accept the fact that I've had a very privileged childhood and upbringing and that has enabled me to be an entrepreneur. I had been working in a number of different sales jobs, and while I was generally pretty good at them, I found it challenging to be constricted in tightly-bound rules and systems.

I didn't have a very clear idea of what I wanted to do, but I took the leap. I think it's really stupid advice to do that unless, like me, you're a white privileged male.

So I just started to write and share my thoughts and ideas and fears and concerns, and ultimately built an audience online. I found that the best way for me to ultimately support myself and also help people in a way that's meaningful to me and not totally soul crushing is through entrepreneurship and through running mastermind groups, which is what I'm focusing on now.

There are a number of challenges that I would say are pretty big, but number one is dealing with this constant impostor syndrome, this notion that I'm not good enough, which probably stems from some sort of childhood trauma or something. Just dealing with that struggle that I don't deserve to build a company or I don't deserve to share something amazing with the world or I don't deserve to support myself through this. Even the really successful entrepreneurs I know deal with that sort of struggle, with that sort of cognitive dissonance. They're doing something amazing that's helping a lot of people but ultimately they still feel like impostors a lot of the time.

Beyond that another huge challenge I deal with is my own ADHD and that's just something that stems from childhood. I've learned to deal with it but I found that when I have too much freedom, it's really challenging to determine the number one thing to focus on, especially when you're all over the place, which I am all the time.

My biggest success is getting people to believe in me and to believe in the work that I'm doing, and that's been really hard for me. For some reason a lot of people believe in me and it's really difficult for me to accept that. I'm getting emotional about this, but it's really difficult for me to wrap my head around the idea that I can create success and I can help people in a really meaningful way that also supports me and does not turn me into a drunk homeless dude. That's been the challenge, but also has been a success because I've been able to convince a lot of people that I can help them. That's been big.

There are a number of pieces of advice I received from some of my great mentors like Dave Kerpen and my close friend Tim Healy. Over the years they have taught me about the importance of giving first, and the importance of just helping people unequivocally and without any sort of expectation. Because if you give with expectation, I think it taints that gift and it just trains people to approach it differently like it's a zero-sum game. And I don't think it is. Life, entrepreneurship, building a business, relationships, it's not a zero-sum game. So I said the best piece of advice is just to give without expectation and to do it constantly. That's one of the major reasons why we're here on earth. It's not for ourselves and not to necessarily find happiness or to discover the meaning of life or anything like that. It's to connect with people. And if you can give something to people and contribute to people and help them with their dreams, then you'll build really, really meaningful connections.

Being aware of your fear is smart. Overcoming it is the mark of a successful person.

- Seth Godin

My name is Nic Gray, the CEO and Co-founder of HyprLoco. I don't want to work for anybody; that is why I became an entrepreneur. And the biggest challenge for me being an entrepreneur was finding a way to live without a paycheck.

The biggest success that I had was raising capital in a very intense environment in Colorado where a majority of the funds are coming in from the (Silicon) Valley. We actually had to move outside of not just Colorado but outside of the States and raise money in Canada.

The best advice that I've ever received actually came from the military and that is: You cannot do everything yourself and you have to rely on that person next to you. So, in business, you obviously need to surround yourself with people who are smarter than you, and that's something that I strive to do. It's even more important to be able to trust them and rely on them.

NIKI
KOUBOURLIS

FOUNDER & CEO
Bold Betties

"MY STARTUP WAS ACCEPTED INTO AN AMAZING ACCELERATOR PROGRAM AND IT MEANS BACKING OUT OF A PRIOR COMMITMENT, LETTING DOWN ONE OF MY BIGGEST SUPPORTERS."

RANA E.
CHO

FOUNDER
Snow Minions

"I HAVE INCREDIBLE TRACTION IN MY BUSINESS AND I STRUGGLE WITH CHRONIC PAIN, PREVENTING ME FROM GROWING AS FAST AS I COULD."

ROBERT
LEVINGSTON

CO-FOUNDER & CEO
Surgical Alternatives

"MY COMPANY IS PARTNERING WITH VCS TO PROPELL BUSINESS TO THE NEXT LEVEL AND I AM IN THE MIDDLE OF A CUSTODY BATTLE FOR MY DAUGHTER."

"OUR BUSINESS (GROOVESHARK) WAS THRIVING WITH 35M USERS, A MILLION A MONTH IN REVENUE, 140 EMPLOYEES AND WE WERE BEING SUED FOR 17 BILLION DOLLARS."

SAM
TARANTINO

**FOUNDER
+ CEO**
chromatic.fm

My name is Sam Tarantino and I am currently the CEO of Chromatic.
FM. My co-founder, Josh Greenberg, and I started out with
Grooveshark, a company we founded to take a stab at solving the
problem of illegal downloads. We built Grooveshark to 35 million users
and $60 million in revenue at one point, and it was beyond our wildest
imaginations as entrepreneurs. All the stories that you hear about success
all at once were coming true for us. So we saw that side of the coin and then
saw the failure side of it when we were sued for 17 billion dollars. We lost it
all. We had to fire 140 employees all at once, then shut the company down
and give everyone their money back.

When we shut down Grooveshark, our plan was to start over and build the
next company together, but that wasn't going to be. Josh died suddenly
at 29. They found him in his bed; he just didn't wake up. It was the first
time I'd ever experienced death and it was a spiral of feeling lost and not
understanding - why did all this happen, what did I do wrong, why am I being
punished?

I moved to Denver and I made a decision that I need to be focusing on the
choice of being happy after being sad all the time. It was just depressing and
it was exhausting and NYC isn't a place people describe as warm and cozy
- it's a harsh place. I had always loved these mountains growing up, I always
loved the outdoors. I thought that one day I'll go raise a family there. The
hardest thing to do is to maintain positivity despite some things collapsing
around you. You can't really affect the things that are happening to you but
you can affect how you interact with them and deal with them. For a while
there I really didn't think I was going to recover.

I focus on athleticism as a way to strengthen myself psychologically and
strengthen my body physically and strengthen my business inspiration. It's
very difficult to build a business when you're not inspired.

I find my best ideas come when I am climbing a fourteener or going down an awesome run and I think "Wait a second, that's how I should approach this problem. I start with me. Am I getting stronger both physically and mentally?" If the answer is yes, then I go to the next concentric circle, which is my group of friends and community. In that group are people who believe in me, people I believe in, and the closer-knit people that bring positivity to my life. The third concentric circle is the more removed one, community service. People I don't know but I can impact in a positive way. It's very easy in the entrepreneurial world, especially in cities like San Francisco and New York, to get caught up in that chase of the bigger apartment, the bigger valuation, the big exits and things like that.

It's been two years since Josh passed, and this time around, I have a much greater sense about the enjoyment of this process versus constantly being stressed out about a future thing that doesn't exist yet. In this second company, we are nine months in and I have gotten more done, the same team has gotten more done than in Grooveshark in two-and-a-half years.

That's just barely focusing on the end result, just enjoying the process and hiring people I really enjoy working with and being inspired by the things that I do. You can create an environment with a tight-knit community. I'm proud that I kept that legacy going.

All my fears came true, and not only did I survive but I feel stronger than I've ever felt. I've come full circle at starting over and being happy again.

It's not what happens to you in life - it's how you respond to what happens to you.

- Eric Thomas

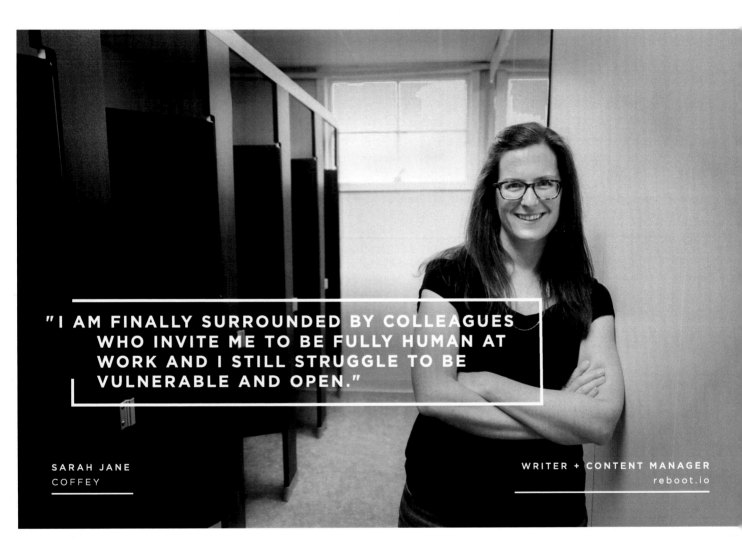

"I AM FINALLY SURROUNDED BY COLLEAGUES WHO INVITE ME TO BE FULLY HUMAN AT WORK AND I STILL STRUGGLE TO BE VULNERABLE AND OPEN."

SARAH JANE
COFFEY

WRITER + CONTENT MANAGER
reboot.io

SAURABH
CHAWLA

CEO & FOUNDER
The Cheetah Express

" AM PROCESSING MORE
ORDERS THAN I EVER
HAVE AND I AM TRYING TO
FIND BALANCE IN LIFE. "

LYNN CLARK PORTRAITS

SHELLEY
JANES

FOUNDER, CEO
SideDoor

"I HAVE NEVER BEEN MORE EXCITED TO HAVE MY OWN BUSINESS AND I FEEL LIKE I AM SEGREGATING MYSELF FROM AN ENTIRE COMMUNITY OF COLLEAGUES."

STACY
MENDITTO

My name is Stacy Menditto, the Founder of Wealth Connection. I became an entrepreneur to escape the corporate rat race, the politics, the who's sleeping with who, the male-dominated world where a female doesn't have the right to speak up. And what I have found with entrepreneurship is I'm living a much more purpose-driven life and what comes with that is total fulfillment.

My biggest challenge is when I am in flow and success begins to happen, it could take an hour or even just a day. The very next day I will wake up and I am heavy in my mind, I am in an obsessive tape recorder telling me not to go do it again. So my biggest challenge is to overcome that fear, that obsession, so I can go ahead and do it again and again and again.

My biggest success is that I have felt being in flow, meaning I can do magical, humongous things that will change this world in a positive way and make an impact.

My best advice I received is: My body does not lie. I use my body, the gut instinct that I feel, the belly flops or even the hair standing up on the back of my neck as signs or indications of what I should do or not do. Your body doesn't lie. My mind definitely can lie, but not my body, and I use that as my guiding force going forward in everything I do.

"I CONNECT PEOPLE WITH SOLUTIONS VERY EASILY AND I DO NOT FEEL LIKE I'M GOOD ENOUGH TO BELIEVE IT IS TRUE."

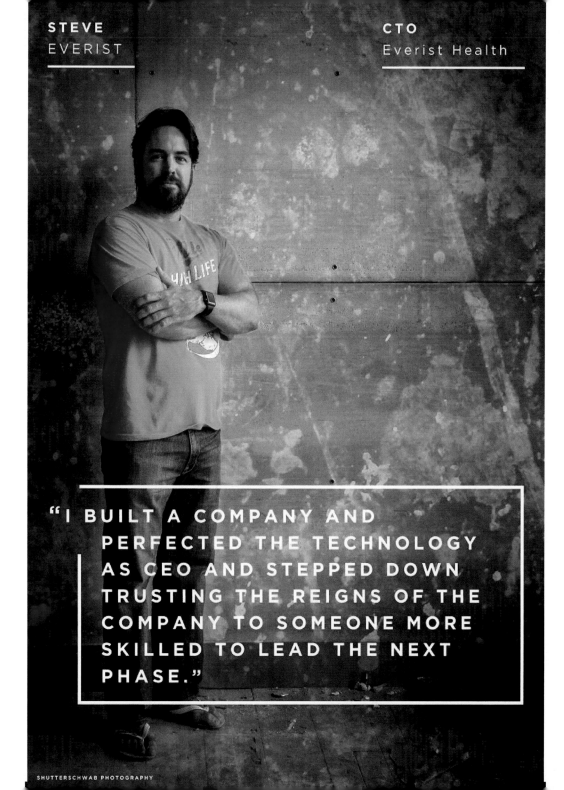

STEVE
EVERIST

CTO
Everist Health

"I BUILT A COMPANY AND PERFECTED THE TECHNOLOGY AS CEO AND STEPPED DOWN TRUSTING THE REIGNS OF THE COMPANY TO SOMEONE MORE SKILLED TO LEAD THE NEXT PHASE."

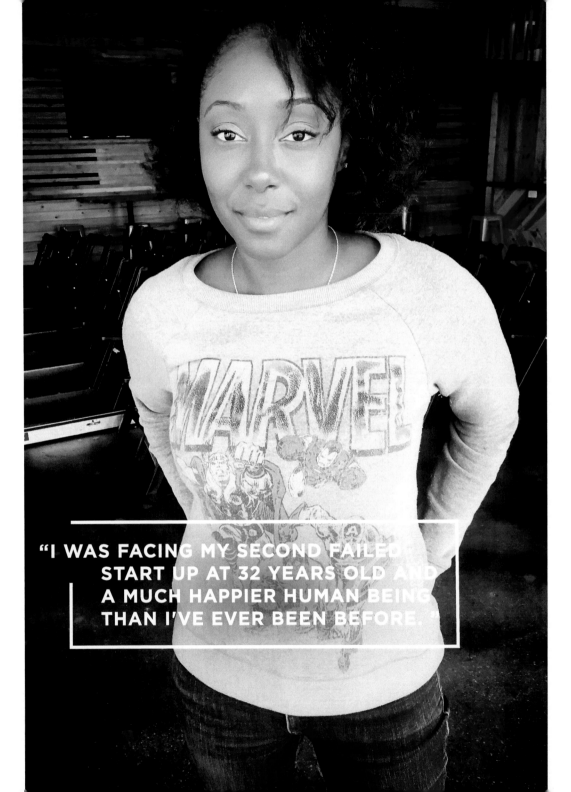

"I WAS FACING MY SECOND FAILED
START UP AT 32 YEARS OLD AND
A MUCH HAPPIER HUMAN BEING
THAN I'VE EVER BEEN BEFORE. "

My name is Tamar Lucien and I am the Founder and CEO of MentalHappy. I originally became an entrepreneur when I decided to take the big leap and quit my job to pursue my own creative passions. I really wanted to not be a part of the day-to-day rat race of driving to work, being on the highway, being on someone else's time clock. I just didn't want to do that anymore. I also wanted freedom to really think and learn. And the third thing is that I wanted to create something from scratch. I didn't know what, but it was a very deep yearning that would wake me up at night; it was my preoccupation all day long.

My biggest challenge today as an entrepreneur is just being in a place where I know and I feel that everything is OK and everything is running on schedule. Often times as entrepreneurs we rush our journey. We rush to get to the finish line, the big win, and we miss everything in between the starting point and the end.

My biggest challenge is just really enjoying the milestones. I know that's kind of ironic because you know I have the company MentalHappy and that's really what we teach people, but it's still something that's very important with me and I work on progressing every day and getting better at it.

My biggest success today would be just my approach to building MentalHappy. This is my third startup, so I'm a three-time founder and my biggest success is the approach, just taking it a little bit more lighthearted, having more fun with it, exploring my creativity in ways that I hadn't before. I think in giving myself permission to be more lax, to be more open, to be more "go with the flow," and allowing things to happen, it's led to our monetary success with the amount of customers that we have in the US and in Canada. It's led to attracting investors and getting funding and the company culture that we're building for the long run.

The best advice I've ever received just in life and in entrepreneurship is the mantra: "Everything is always working out for you." When the mantra says "everything" it means everything. So even your failures, even the things that you think haven't worked out, even the things that you think, "Oh gosh this is so horrible you know I'll never recover from this," even those moments are conspiring some way, redirecting you some way, to the path that you're supposed to be on.

CEO + FOUNDER
mental happy

"I TELL MY CLIENTS WHO WANT TO HAVE LASTING LOVE TO FIRST FIND YOU, AND I AM STILL TRYING TO FIND ME EVERY DAY."

My name is Teena Evert and I'm the Founder and creator of Ignite Love Now. I became an entrepreneur to be able to live my life creatively and position myself in the world to help as many people as possible, particularly women. I work with high-achieving women who feel unfulfilled in their love life. They want to learn how to build a healthy relationship and have love that lasts. My biggest challenge has been my own life really; my story and learning how to lead as a woman. I grew up during the height of the Women's Liberation movement in America's heartland. And there was a misogynistic undercurrent that ran through the generations of my family. Divorces occurred like dominoes in the 1980s. This fueled a lot of anger and disconnection between the men and the women. This is also what ignited my desire to create something different for my future. I learned really hard lessons at a very young age from the messages that I took in from my family about not being valued as a woman; being weak, incompetent or inferior to men. For example, it was not uncommon for my mom to be scrambling around in the kitchen to get dinner on the table just in time for my father to come home after a long day at work. Or the time when we went on a family road trip to visit my grandparents in Florida and my dad insisted on driving the entire way because he didn't believe my mom was a competent driver. I was constantly observing women being told to play small if not being told to be silent altogether. And although I didn't realize it at the time, I think I became a marriage and family therapist and addictions counselor and a relationship coach to better understand myself, my family and relationships in general.

One of my biggest successes is that I have been honored to work with many people struggling with mental health issues, complex trauma, post-traumatic stress disorder, marital problems, relational trauma and on and on. But the one thing that everyone I've worked with has had in common, irrespective of how much tragedy they have lived through or how much privilege they've had is that they all carry around pain from their relationships, particularly their intimate partner relationships.

The best advice that I've received is to learn how to let go of whatever mindsets or whatever habits I carry around that get in my way of being successful, successful in love, successful in business, successful in choosing a life that I want to live and to learn how to receive and lead authentically with love.

All that we are is a result of what we have thought.

- *Buddha*

TIM
WOLTERS

FOUNDER & CEO
RoundPegg

"WE'RE HITTING REVENUE
TARGETS AND I'M DRIVING
MY DAUGHTER'S CAR TO
STAY AFLOAT."

TOMA
BEDOLLA

My name is Toma Bedolla and I'm the founder and CEO of a community engagement platform called House of Genius. I prefer the title "Chief Disrupter." Entrepreneurship was a natural fit for my talents my ambitions, my visions, my delusions. I've had a sort of problem-solver nature from the beginning, so I embarked on entrepreneurship after a career in the corporate world and a brief sabbatical on the PGA Tour.

The biggest challenge of being an entrepreneur is a really considerable lack of understanding of what it means to be an entrepreneur and the challenges that are part of that path.

My biggest success as an entrepreneur is inspiring other people who worked on projects, not the success of the organization itself. I feel I have leveraged servant leadership to empower and embolden unbelievably brilliant, beautiful and talented spirits across the number of projects and teams that I've had the good fortune to lead to think bigger than just the paycheck and the traditional view of what it means to have a career.

I think the best piece and most broadly applicable advice that I've ever received is to try to apply discovery-based learning to every step of the process. If you're not smarter or you don't understand something more than you did before you embarked on a particular action, task, or exercise, then what are you doing? Make sure that you know what it is you're trying to achieve every step of the way. My advice to other entrepreneurs is to better respect the value you bring when your contribution is passion and time. Your time is valuable; a minute to you is the same as it is for a billionaire. And that's very difficult for human beings to embrace, but it's absolutely true. Approach every situation, especially when you're seeking funding, by recognizing that your time and their time is of equal value. Besides, they put their pants on one leg at a time just like you.

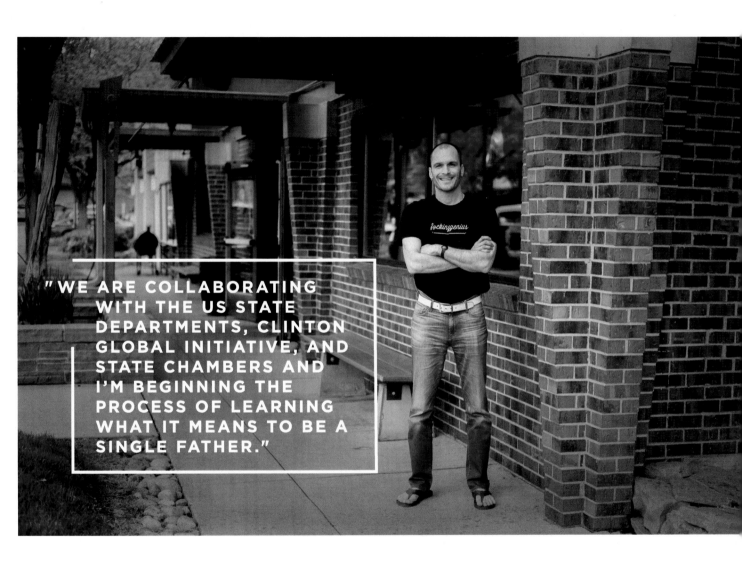

"WE ARE COLLABORATING WITH THE US STATE DEPARTMENTS, CLINTON GLOBAL INITIATIVE, AND STATE CHAMBERS AND I'M BEGINNING THE PROCESS OF LEARNING WHAT IT MEANS TO BE A SINGLE FATHER."

"I QUIT MY JOB AS A COLLEGE PROFESSOR, STARTED A PRODUCTION COMPANY WITH MY STUDENTS AND I HAVE BI-POLAR DISORDER."

TRAVIS
BOCKENSTEDT

CO-FOUNDER
fourth wall
productions

My name's Travis Bockenstedt. I am a Denver transplant from Strawberry Point, Iowa, a small farming community. I came to Denver to launch a startup company called Fourth Wall Productions with two other co-founders. I decided to become an entrepreneur after teaching in higher education for five years as a college professor.

We had a group of five students who came together for a senior capstone project to create a documentary. And the students who did this documentary project were thought of as the underdogs in the department. They were all awesome, amazing students, but they may not have been the most vocal students about their accomplishments and I don't think a lot of people expected them to succeed. But as I started working on their senior capstone project, I started to realize that this group of young people had something very special in common and that was the fact that they were true creators, true artists, beautiful storytellers, and they just needed a platform to do it.

And when their documentary was finished, they came up to me and asked if I'd be interested in doing a startup company with them. That was two years ago and I thought it was a perfect opportunity to do it. I've been wanting to start a business my whole life and I've been waiting to find the right group of people to work with to do it. Year one was a challenge. We were trying to start a company while I was still a full-time college professor in Iowa. We had the majority of our crew in Denver, and I spent a good part of the year flying back and forth to Denver to help mentor and build this company, and it was a huge challenge for us. I think everything that could have gone wrong went wrong in that first year. We were not jiving as a group, we had different ideas of where we wanted to go. A year into these ups and downs and successes and sadness and tears we had to have that "come to Jesus" moment where three of our members left the company. It was the closest thing I've ever experienced to divorce. My parents were divorced but I've never gone through divorce personally.

At the end of the day, I realized that I had to break up with some of my best friends, people I love and care about and shared everything with. I think it was one of the hardest revelations I ever had in my life that I would have to have a conversation with three people that I love to ask them to reconsider being a part of our company, that this was an opportunity for them to leave.

And looking back, after that day I literally thought the company was gone, everything we were working for would be finished, and for me it was going to be a huge embarrassment. It's not something you want to do and I think that was my first moment in feeling defeat within a startup, the fact that I couldn't keep a team together, the fact that we completely lost track of where we were going.

But there was a little bit of light at the end of the tunnel. I was lucky enough to have two co-founders by my side the whole time who were able to help us find and bring in some new talented people who would make Fourth Wall a company we could never imagine, and it's been magical to watch.

And it goes back to the whole essence of why being an entrepreneur is important to me, because you can make an impact on other people's lives. My mission going ahead from there was to be a mentor and to help people find their calling in life and to help others succeed. The only thing that keeps me going is seeing my team succeed, to see them smile, to see them win, to have a client say, "That's the best thing I've ever seen" and have tears come to their eyes. I come to work every single day only because I want to see our entire team succeed.

I think our biggest success as a team so far has nothing to do with how much money we've made or haven't made. I think our biggest successes are little things that we get excited about. For instance, the fact that we just got health care a few days ago and that as a business we can pay for 80% of our employees' health care. And another thing that's been a huge success for us is that we've been able to come together and have honest conversations as owners and with our employees that I've never had with another company before. We sit around the table and we talk about our financial situation and about where we want to go, and to let everyone have a say in where Fourth Wall wants to go is what makes our company special.

I think my only role as the president of the company is to help everybody envision their ideas. I'm constantly asking everyone, "What can I do to help support you?"

I'm the coffee runner in the business. I'm the one who goes to Starbucks and picks up coffee to keep our team going. That's not an intern job, that's the president's job in the company. I believe my job to help us succeed is to sit down and pull each and every one of our team members aside, and have a conversation with them and ask the simple question, "How are you doing today?" And go beyond that. I just I don't think there's a business if we don't have a healthy team, if we don't have passionate people who believe in our cause and who believe in the people who are trying to build this business.

I received some great advice the time I quit my first job. It was from my boss at a TV station in Iowa. I was working in sales at the time and I loved my boss. He was one of the best mentors I ever had. And he looked at me and he said, "Travis, I want you to realize that the grass is never greener on the other side."

And I know that's a bit of a cliché, but when you're in the startup world, the grass sometimes isn't even there on the other side. You go into a new project, or you go into a new adventure and you arrive and there's a desert and weeds. There's no grass at all.

And I think sometimes as entrepreneurs we need to start looking at the grass on the other side and deciding: how are we going to make this grow, how are we going to make it better, how we are going to root it all up and start over again?

"I BUILT THE COMPANIES I ALWAYS WANTED AND IT DIDN'T PROVIDE THE MEANING I THOUGHT IT WOULD WHEN MY FAMILY SEPARATED."

WADE
ROSEN

My name is Wade Rosen and I'm the CEO of Enjoywishlist and Thrivepass. Enjoywishlist is an experiential rewards and recognition platform for companies and Thrivepass is a benefits platform specializing in well-being and pre-tax benefits for companies.

I became an entrepreneur when I was living in Madrid. I had just finished my MBA at IE Business school and I met my business partner Andreas Deptolla. We were wrestling with the idea of going back and becoming investment bankers or strategic consultants, but we knew that if we didn't start our company at this point that our lives would get in the way. So we decided to move to Boulder and start a company that was about as far away from those fields as you can get.

The biggest challenge that I face as an entrepreneur is balance. I've never been good at maintaining balance in anything that I've done. When I commit to something I usually jump into it fully, to the detriment of a lot of other things in my life. When we started the company, Andreas Deptolla, Charlie Shen and I were completely committed. As a result, my own personal needs, the needs of my family, and lots of other things hit the back burner. I think that is one of the reasons my family ended up separating.

As far as the biggest success, there are two main successes - the first came really early. I chose great partners in Andreas and Charles. There were years when, if one of us would have backed out, both companies would have collapsed. We stuck with it, and we're now five years into it. It has been just amazing to have them along for the whole time.

The other success is the teams that we built. I love the people I get to work with every day. They're interesting, smart, funny, caring, really kind people, and coming to work is often times the best part of my days. When I look back, those are the two things that are the biggest successes for Wishlist and Thrivepass.

The best advice I ever received was actually from my father at a young age. He told me not to be a lawyer. I say that jokingly, although I have had to read so many contracts over the past five years. I'm definitely glad that I didn't go into that field – I would be doing that twelve hours a day.

My advice to other entrepreneurs is to not let their self-worth and happiness get tied up in the success of the company. While it's something that we all think we know, the reality is when you're involved in it every day for as many hours as you are, it's really difficult to not let that happen. I didn't realize that was the case for me until my daughter moved to Germany with her mother two years ago. Then all of a sudden, all the things that seemed so incredibly important paled in comparison to that. I realized then that I had been so worried about the success of the company that I had let the truly important things in life slip.

A man is but the product of his thoughts.
What he thinks, he becomes.

- Gandhi

ACKNOWLEDGMENTS

Community isn't built alone. It's collaborative and many people made Impact Founder and this book possible. The book wouldn't even be an idea without the early adapters and numerous founders who initially trusted me in telling their raw, real and sometimes vulnerable stories. They sat with me, a complete stranger, and trusted my vision. For the founders who continue to share, I have immeasurable gratitude.

Amy Baglan. I remember when we met at Denver Startup Week 2013, and I knew there was something magical about her. Maybe it was her side shave and idealistic view on creating mindfulness in the online dating space, but maybe it was that she would become my best friend. She's sat through many of my ideas and supported them with introductions, advice and listening. When I started Impact Founder, I was living with Amy. We were walking her dog, Bali, and I shared about my idea to build the Impact Founder project photo exhibit.

Amy Collette. Early on with Impact Founder I said I would write a book, but it kept being pushed back and put on the back burner. Thank you for coming to me and sharing your belief in my book at precisely the right time. Your expertise, coaching, and editing has made this experience quite seamless and enjoyable.

Brock Predovich. I hadn't known Brock well before this project. We met for the second time and I floated this idea to him. He opened up, shared openly and vulnerably about his own experience. He was so touched, moved and inspired that he offered a location for our first photo shoot.

Carly Hana. You are an inspiration to me. Thank you for all the long phone calls allowing me to empty out my bucket. Each and every one of those times I called needing an ear allowed me the energy necessary to put this all on paper. Who you are inspires me daily. Thank you for finding me, supporting me, loving me. You lift me up when I am down and remind me of my commitment.

Charlie Hessler & Jennifer Infantino. Thankful for you stepping up and collaborating on the design and installation of our initial exhibit at Galvanize Platte Campus.

Danielle Norris. From our first meeting at Black Eye Coffee to walks around Sloan's Lake, you instantly saw my vision and generously took Impact Founder on as a client. Thank you for endless hours of support, and for picking me up when I had feelings of giving up on our plan.

David Novin. Thank you for stepping in at the last moment even when things were hectic in your life to create "the perfect photo" of me for the book. I know I have high standards and you really just rolled with it. Your photography is awesome and I don't think I said that enough.

Eddie Knight. Thank you for always trusting, believing and laughing with me. Designing this book with you has been fun. Being friends for 18 years is no small feat. Thank you for hanging in all these years and playing design with all my wacky ideas. Thank you for trusting in me.

Josh Whitaker. Thankful for your endless, thankless hours building our first website.

Krista Algrim. I hadn't met Krista when she put her neck out to host Impact Founder's initial exhibit at Galvanize. She saved the day, and stood for hosting our exhibit when our location fell through. The conversation was new, and no one wanted to talk about 'depressing things'. Thank you, Krista, for standing for Impact Founder's exhibit. It was BOLD and generous.

Lane Ostrow. There are people you meet along the way who are an inspiration. They "get it". Thank you for pushing me when I needed a nudge, and for contributing to this process as if it were your own.

Lisa Schwab, Lynn Clark. I am appreciative for all I saw and didn't see that went into creating the pictures for the inaugural exhibit. I remember scouting the location full of excitement and the passion, excitement that we shared. I hope you know the immense gratitude I have for the enthusiasm, effort, support, artistry and creativity that went into the exhibit.

Lizelle VanVuuren. A huge shout out for accidentally saving me from a terrible name for Impact Founder - so terrible I don't remember it. Fist bump for the initial brainstorming sessions and for providing years of Women Who Startup events so I could sponge up all the necessary details to have the gumption, the knowledge and support of women who have come before me.

Mike Biselli. He jumped on the Impact Founder train early. I sat across from him passionately talking about Impact Founder and within moments he was real, vulnerable and I was in tears. Mike, thank you for all of the support from day one. It is a distinct pleasure to have you alongside me in this journey, my friend.

My TMLP Team. Thank you for listening to me as my commitment, and nothing short of it. For loving me how I am and how I am not; for being a stand for me to complete this book and to create the life of my dreams

My Community. Back to the community support. I'd be remiss if I didn't mention how incredibly lucky I am to have integrated into the community that comprises the Denver/Boulder startup scene. Denver has such an inclusive community and they have been alongside me in building Impact Founder from the beginning: Mike Biselli, Lizelle Van Vuuren, **Aj Cohen, Galvanize, Emilie Kitner, Dave Mayer, John Schnipkoweit, Alexandra Weiner, Sally J Spencer, Josh Andersson, Denver Startup Week, The Commons on Champa, the Downtown Denver Partnership.**

My family has been an instrumental piece of building alongside me, brick by brick, idea by idea, since before I can recall. Throughout the career changes, the next shiny idea, and feeling like I didn't 'fit the mold', my parents have always been my biggest supporters. My dad, **Bruce Darga** has enrolled all the people closest to him into what I am doing as I keep climbing. He's procured votes, clicks and kickstarter dollars. I don't think I have a bigger fan. I know without a doubt how proud he is of me. My mom, **Sharon Darga**, is my rock. She is my board to bounce ideas off of, the person I call with news - good or bad. She's created multiple excel spreadsheets, listened to hours of stories, transcribed, edited, and provided endless hours of love and support. She's gotten excited about many small celebrations with me. I hit the jackpot with my parents, and realize how lucky I am to have their support. They believe that anything I set my mind to is possible, and even when I stop believing, they are there to remind me. This book is theirs as much as it is mine.

I am in gratitude to my big sis, **Kim Darga**. She's a steady, loving, nurturing force of nature and support in my life. My brother-in-law, **Andrew Needham**, is an inspiration. His book, written over 10 years, reminds me it's not always simple and a masterpiece takes time. **Jack and Ray**, from the moment I saw you run down the hall in your apartment to say hi to me when you were 2 years old, you have shown me how simple unconditional love is, thank you. I love you both back.

For my grandmother, **Muriel**, who has passed. You have pushed me past my boundaries. Having you support my dreams and be at my graduation from the Journalism program at Michigan State University while you were sick meant the world to me. I love you and I know you believed in me.

ABOUT THE AUTHOR

Kristin Darga, Founder of Impact Founder™, is an executive coach who guides and supports entrepreneurs to break the code of what's holding them back from success. After her ex-boyfriend almost took his life and she heard about a number of founder suicides, Kristin took action and created Impact Founder, a global multi-media movement to build a community where people get real about entrepreneurship. This growing community supports and empowers entrepreneurs to combat isolation through connection and support each other through the struggles to make a lasting impact.

For more information on Impact Founder, or to be featured as an Impact Founder, please visit: www.impactfounder.com

To book Kristin for interviews, keynotes, or coaching email: impactfounderproject@gmail.com